Texas Art and a Wildcatter's Dream

NUMBER NINE:

The Joe and Betty Moore Texas Art Series

Texas Art and a Wildcatter's Dream

Edgar B. Davis and the San Antonio Art League

WILLIAM E. REAVES, JR.

Foreword by Cecilia Steinfeldt
Afterword by Richard Casagrande

Texas A&M University Press
College Station

The paper used in this book meets the minimum requirements

of the American National Standard for Permanence

of Paper for Printed Library Materials, Z39.48-1984.

Binding materials have been chosen for durability.

Library of Congress Cataloging-in-Publication Data

Reaves, William E.

    Texas art and a wildcatter's dream : Edgar B. Davis and the San Antonio Art League /
William E. Reaves, Jr. ; afterword by Richard Casagrande. — 1st ed.

        p.   cm. — (The Joe and Betty Moore Texas art series ; no. 9)

    Includes bibliographical references and index.

    ISBN 0-89096-812-8 (cloth : alk. paper). — ISBN 0-89096-820-9 (pbk. : alk. paper)

    1. Wild flowers in art. 2. Regionalism in art—Texas. 3. Painting—Competitions—Texas.
4. Painting, American—Texas. 5. Painting, Modern—20th century—Texas. 6. Davis,
Edgar B. (Edgar Byrum), b. 1873—Art patronage. I. Title. II. Series.

ND1402.6.R43   1998

758´.42´09764—dc21   97-24600

                                                                         CIP

*To Linda, scientist, educator, wife, and friend.
With deepest love and admiration.*

Contents

Illustrations

Plates

Foreword

In *Texas Art and a Wildcatter's Dream: Edgar B. Davis and the San Antonio Art League,* William Reaves has provided us with a sympathetic account of an unusual man, Edgar B. Davis, as well as a concise history of the Texas Wildflower Competitive Exhibitions engendered by Davis's interest in the arts.

These exhibitions were a milestone in the saga of Texas art history and have never before been explored in depth. That they occurred at all was the consequence of Davis's exceptional character and altruistic philosophy. They had a significant impact on the arts in Texas not only because of the munificent prize moneys but also because they enlivened the local art scene by attracting noted artists from out of state.

Many of the artists represented in those competitions remained in San Antonio and contributed to its cultural milieu. Harry Anthony DeYoung was one who chose to make the city his home. Originally from Illinois, he had been educated at the University of Illinois and at the Art Institute of Chicago. Aside from being a skilled draftsman and consummate painter, he was an excellent teacher. After DeYoung's arrival in San Antonio, the Great Depression curtailed commissions and prizes, and he turned his talents to teaching. He survived by organizing classes in the city and held summer sessions in West Texas and northern Mexico. DeYoung's contributions may have seemed trivial at the time, but his artistic philosophy was instilled in his many students and contributed to the growth of art in the state as well as the city.

Dawson Dawson-Watson was another artist who was lured to San Antonio by the Davis competitions. His influence on the local scene was not through his teaching but due to his many exhibitions and involvement in regional art organizations. Born in England, his background was continental, and his views reflected the more modern idioms of impressionism and semi-abstractionism. He won the $5,000 prize in the first Davis competition for his impressionistic interpretation of cactus entitled *The Glory of the Morning.* This painting, plus many others with the wildflower theme, sparked a frenzied effort by many amateur painters to interpret the Texas floral countryside. Most of these paintings were mediocre, but some have survived as adequate visual concepts of the vanishing Texas scene.

José Arpa, a Spaniard, had already made San Antonio his home, and his paintings always won acclaim in the competitions, notably in the categories of cotton fields and ranch life. His nephew, Xavier Gonzalez, in his teens during the competitions, went on in later life to become probably the most successful of the competitors. He became internationally known as a painter for his distinctively expressionistic style, for his three-dimensional creations, and for his immense and moving murals. He was truly a Renaissance man.

There are countless others who made their contributions to the Davis competitions and who are thoroughly recognized in William Reaves's narrative. Viewed today, the paintings seem somewhat dated and conventional. However, as time goes by and interest increases in regional art, these paintings are proving to be of immense importance. They are typical of the contemporary art of the period and reflect a quality of realism that is in direct opposition to the extreme abstractionism of today's painting. They are again being appreciated for their competent craftsmanship, honest interpretation, and genre subject matter.

The Witte Museum in San Antonio was chosen by Davis to host these important exhibitions. Established in 1926, the museum was in its infancy when the competitions began, and the responsibility and prestige of organizing these competitions provided a golden opportunity for the institution to spread its untried wings. It proved equal to the task largely due to the efforts of Eleanor Onderdonk, art curator, and Ethel Tunstall Drought, San Antonio Art League president. These endeavors were augmented by Ellen Schulz, museum director, and the rest of the Witte staff.

But Edgar B. Davis was the guiding light, with his staunch support and unselfish distribution of wealth. He may be considered eccentric, but he was a man of quiet determination and inflexible faith. He chose to share his affluence as well as his beliefs and in doing so benefitted the museum, the city, and the state. We are now indebted to William Reaves, who has meticulously researched this project and has furnished us with a clear, concise overview of the extraordinary wildflower competitions, as well as a compassionate interpretation of a unique man.

CECILIA STEINFELDT
Curator Emeritus, Witte Museum

Acknowledgments

In any venture such as this there are many individuals who give much needed support and assistance, without which it would be impossible to achieve a satisfactory conclusion. This is especially true in the case of this particular book, and acknowledgments of these special efforts are in order.

It was Tom Pilkington, University scholar and professor at Tarleton State University, who helped me muster up the courage to proceed with this project in the first place. Despite a full and challenging schedule, Dr. Pilkington took the time to review my initial proposal for this book. His encouraging feedback and advice on how to proceed motivated me to move forward with the project. In addition to Dr. Pilkington, many of my former Tarleton colleagues offered timely assistance. President Dennis McCabe supported the project with great enthusiasm, and my former boss, Ronnie Sheppard, granted me the flexibility and latitude to complete the research. Jenny Green supplied invaluable clerical support, and Holli Howard was always there to lend a hand as a trusty research assistant.

I also owe a tremendous debt of gratitude to the board of directors of the San Antonio Art League. They have been delightful and cooperative partners throughout the entire venture. Board Chair Nancy Bacon has offered leadership to the project, and former board member Blaire Carnahan served as one of the earliest and strongest advocates of the book. Norma Champlin, a longtime league member and volunteer "curator" of the Davis collection, offered critical assistance in the research stages of the project. Her firsthand knowledge of the league's archives, coupled with her acquaintance with the art and artists of the collection, proved to be extremely helpful. Her devotion to the particular works in the Davis collection came to be a source of inspiration to me, and she remains, in my eyes, the most knowledgeable person today with regard to these paintings. Her successor at the art league, Lillian Gonzales, also offered timely and gracious assistance.

The Genealogical and Historical Society of Caldwell County, likewise, was a wonderful partner. Their collection of papers on Edgar B. Davis was a key resource for research. Eva Wilson and husband, Dr. Francis Wilson, were eager compatriots in this undertaking. They devoted many hours to locating Davis materials and memorabilia. Through them I had the pleasure of meeting Catherine Davis, one of "Edgar B.'s" former secretaries. This warm and personable lady supplied important materials and offered firsthand insights into Davis's work and philosophy during a marvelous interview at her home.

A grant from the Summerlee Foundation enabled us to document the files of the art league and to photograph the entire Davis collection. Foundation executive John Crain was most helpful and gave sound professional advice on the submission of our proposal. Dr. Ron Tyler, Executive Director of the Texas State Historical Society and a scholar of Texas art, took time from his demanding schedule to critique our proposal to the Summerlee Foundation and offered useful insights for refinement.

A special acknowledgment is also due Riley Froh, the Luling author who has written wonderful biographies of Edgar B. Davis. I was able to build on his excellent work in crafting my own story of Davis, couched within the context of these fine art competitions. My associations with Riley in the course of this project have shown me that he truly is a gentleman and a scholar in the finest sense of the words.

To Cecilia Steinfeldt I give my highest thanks for providing the foreword for this publication. She graciously undertook the task even with her writing arm constrained while in recuperation from shoulder surgery. I am deeply grateful for her time and her contributions to this book, especially under these circumstances. In her long and productive career, she has set a standard for scholarship in the arts and material culture of this state. As a longtime admirer of her work, I was greatly honored that she lent her expertise to this project.

I was honored also that Rick Casagrande would offer the afterword for this book. His observations on the paintings in the Davis Collection of the San Antonio Art League are poignant and incisive. No one is better suited to comment on the nuances of the Davis Collection than is he, as a member of the art league's board and an independent art appraiser and teacher. I am indebted to Rick for taking time from his busy schedule to provide a professional critique of these important paintings.

My sincere thanks to all these wonderful folks, and to yet others whose efforts I may have failed to document here. I think that together we have been able to tell an interesting story that adds to the rich cultural history of this state.

Texas Art and a Wildcatter's Dream

CHAPTER ONE

An Introduction and Backdrop

In the years 1927 through 1929, a series of art competitions and exhibitions were held in San Antonio, Texas, under the auspices of the San Antonio Art League. The Texas Wildflower Competitive Exhibitions, as they were officially entitled, were the brainchild of one of the state's most curious and legendary oil wildcatters— the illustrious Edgar B. Davis of Luling, Texas, and Brockton, Massachusetts. Bolstered by record-setting cash purchase prizes, generous publicity, and national exhibitions, the Davis competitions, as they became popularly known, proved to be among the most significant cultural events in Texas during those formative years of the twentieth century. They were instrumental in forging the state's emerging art community and catapulting Texas art into the national limelight of the day.

Although an important part of the state's cultural and artistic history, these art exhibitions remain virtually unknown today and are long overdue as subjects of serious research and documentation. This book, therefore, contributes a much needed history of these compelling art events. It provides a record of these unique contests, depicting the critical and popular significance of these grand events, and illustrates, for the first time, the complete collection of prizewinning paintings from the competitions, which today hang largely unheralded in the galleries of the San Antonio Art League.

The fact that the Texas Wildflower Competitive Exhibitions are inextricably bound to the life and legend of Edgar B. Davis makes these events even more captivating and historically significant. Therefore, to a great extent this is also a story about the contest patron, Edgar B. Davis, a transplanted "Yankee trader," who parlayed entrepreneurial genius and unshakable faith into one of the oil business's great wildcatting fortunes and who graced his adopted state of Texas with this art legacy.

When the twenties roared in Texas, Edgar B. Davis was among the wealthiest and most influential Texans. He was a self-made oil man. A wildcatter who drilled "as wild a wildcat as one ever encounters," Davis achieved great prominence in the state's oil industry in the face of almost unbelievable odds.[1] A deeply spiritual man, equally unorthodox in both his philosophy and philanthropy, he was heralded as one of the remarkable personalities of his generation. Yet Davis, like the art contests he sponsored, has faded into relative obscurity today. At the time, however, he was perhaps one of the few Texas millionaires who could have conceptualized and carried out the competitions. He was worldly and sophisticated, imbued with a deep appreciation for the fine arts and a special affection for Texas wildflowers. Consequently, he became the perfect patron for these phenomenal art events, and as was his style, he saw to it that they were carried out with great flair and notable class. It was he who envisioned a national art competition in which leading American painters of the day would assemble in Texas to vie for the honor of best capturing the beauty and grandeur of the state's abundant wildflowers. The purchase prizes that he endowed for the contest were, in fact, the most generous that had ever been offered in America for single works up to that time.[2] These lucrative prizes did indeed attract to Texas a large contingent of the nation's most prominent artists for the first time in the state's history. Initially they came to paint the floral subjects and later, as Davis expanded the contest categories, to portray the ranching and cotton industries of the Lone Star State.

While the contest's prizes attracted national artists to Texas, the awards for indigenous artists helped to acquaint the populace with the work of important Texas painters of the period, who were at the time painting and displaying their works throughout the state in disparate art colonies in San Antonio, Dallas, Houston, and El Paso. The exhibits of these paintings helped to inaugurate the newly opened Witte Museum in San Antonio and became by far the largest and most popular art exhibitions of their day, displaying over three hundred works representative of some 135 artists and drawing almost 80,000 viewers over the three years of the competitions.[3] The winning paintings were purchased by Davis and donated to the art league. They were annually toured in traveling exhibitions throughout the state, and winners were exhibited each year in New York at Columbia University. For better or for worse, the Davis competitions provided Texas art and artists their first broadscale exposure and critical review. As such, the competitions fostered a heightened awareness and support of the visual arts in Texas and set the stage for the important regionalist schools that were to follow in the thirties and forties.

At the time of the Davis competitions, Texas could claim no great painting tradition, although there had been steady growth in the arts beginning in the latter decades of the nineteenth century. Both the late Jerry Bywaters and the contemporary art historian William H. Goetzmann have observed that this dearth of early artistic record is surprising, given Texas' dramatic and romantic history.[4] In assessing the reasons why Texas was a late bloomer in the nation's art circles, Goetzmann offers the following insights:

> Texas had no Missouri River, hence no 3,000 miles of scenic panorama for artists to paint from steamboats and keelboats. No picturesque Oregon trail crossed its terrain. Majestic mountain ranges like the Rockies and the Sierras were mere mirages on the vast emptiness of the Staked Plains. Texas had no Yellowstone or

Yosemite, and its Grand Canyon, the Palo Duro, drew only the genius of Georgia O'Keefe and certainly few tourists, so remote was its location. The railroads did not pay photographers and artists to picture Texas, as did the Union Pacific, the Denver and Rio Grande, and the Great Northern that crossed the Rockies. The Santa Fe employed great painters like Thomas Moran to work up splendid scenes of the Grand Canyon. It also employed the Taos Society of Artists and the Santa Fe group to paint an endless number of pictures of Pueblo Indian culture. Meanwhile, the Southern Pacific which crossed Texas on the way to California employed artists to tout only its California scenery and mission culture. To the Southern Pacific, the huge Texas missions like those in San Antonio were not important. . . .[5]

Writing in 1935, Esse Forrester O'Brien offered at least one more plausible explanation for the state's slow course of artistic development in her treatise *Art and Artists of Texas,* in which she observes, "What civilized man painted the first picture in Texas will probably never be known judging from the following incident related as an historical fact: 'In the days when Indians ruled the land, the story goes that while an unknown artisan was yet carving on the great door of LaSalle's fort on Lavaca Bay, the Indians smote him down.' Art is especially slow where scalping is in style."[6]

Indeed, research has now shown us that the very first historical image of the state created by a professional artist, done in 1763 and entitled *The Destruction of Mission San Sabá in the Province of Texas and the Martyrdom of the Fathers Alone Gerald de Terrors, Joseph Santiesteban,* depicted the massacre of these Spanish missionaries by hostile Comanches within the province of Texas.[7] Visiting Texas in 1834 to record the life and customs of the Comanches, the famous American artist and chronicler of Native American culture George Catlin wrote that "art may mourn when these peoples are swept from the earth, and the artists of future ages may look in vain for another race so picturesque in their costumes, their weapons, their colours, their manly games and their chase."[8] While the artist may have mourned their passing, it would have been difficult to have found many pioneer Texians who shared Catlin's sentiments, at least with regard to this particular tribe.

Whether scalping remained in style for too long, or whether due to the state's geography, nineteenth-century Texas was largely overlooked in the emergent body of American landscape painting. Other than a few soldier-artists or survey-artists, the vast and diverse terrain of Texas had failed to attract the early American artists of western landscape and frontier life, such as Albert Bierstadt and others, whose majestic scenes of the Rockies and the Pacific Northwest gained favor in the East. Besides this lack of artists from outside its borders, there were only a few indigenous painters residing within the Republic and early Texas who could record the state on canvas. Even had there been more artists during this period, there were few citizens with sufficient resources and appreciation to acquire their works. As Frances Battaile Fisk has noted, "the Texans of earlier generations were too occupied with the development of material resources, following the struggle for independence, to have any leisure for the enjoyment of beauty." She quoted James Chillman, one of the leading proponents of Houston's art colony and an early professor at Rice Institute, that "it is not possible to have an age of great art and artistry until the people of that age have reached a reasonable degree of material security."[9]

Indeed, the economic viability of the state was thwarted early on because of Texas' troubled transformation from republic to statehood to secession to Reconstruction, making it further difficult for the arts to gain a foothold in the mid–nineteenth century. Beginning in the late 1870s, however, the state experienced a sustained period of economic growth and prosperity that continued relatively unabated into the second decade of the new century. The boom began with cotton, progressed on the strength of the cattle industry, and oil was added at the turn of the century. Together, these formed the triumvirate of industries that would supply the necessary wealth and leisure for Texans to embrace the arts.

In the first advance of Texas artists, San Antonio has the distinction of attracting the most accomplished and prolific of these. Theodore Gentilz, a draftsman for Castro's nearby colony, was in the city by 1844. He executed many important paintings, laying down on canvas some of the earliest and most important artistic records of the state. Gentilz had the distinction of being the first to paint the Alamo, completing his work only four years after the great battle on that site.[10] Seth Eastman was stationed in the city from 1848 through most of 1849, and he too offered important renditions of San Antonio and its environs. In the late 1840s, even the city's sheriff, former Texas Ranger William M. G. Samuel, was moved to try his hand with the brush and produced an interesting series of naive paintings of San Antonio, as well as portraits of famous Texas patriots.[11]

The 1850s brought an influx of German immigrants to the San Antonio vicinity, including Hermann Lungkwitz and Richard Petri, two brothers-in-law who settled in the nearby town of Fredericksburg. Both Lungkwitz and Petri were excellent draftsmen, schooled in fine German academies in Dresden. They began to paint the Hill Country landscape and to offer intriguing vignettes of the daily life of early settlers as well as studies of the Native American tribes that frequented the area at the time of their arrival. Petri died shortly after his arrival in Texas, tragically drowning in the Pedernales River near his home, thus cutting short the career of one of the state's earliest artists in residence. Lungkwitz, however, eventually moved to San Antonio after the Civil War where he conducted an art school, established one of the state's first photography studios, and continued to paint strong landscapes that featured the city and the Hill Country terrain of central Texas.

Unquestionably, San Antonio's art community benefitted immensely from the wave of European immigrants settling the area during this period. The region gained many fine artisans and, more important, secured a new generation of residents who valued and appreciated the arts, nurturing their growth in the city during the middle years of the century. San Antonio was rapidly becoming the premiere art center in the newly established state of Texas, a position the city would hold through the decade of the twenties and the time of the Davis competitions.

As early as 1882, *The Alamo City Guide* touted the city's burgeoning art community, stating in one of its articles, "San Antonio is fast becoming celebrated for the culture and refinement of its citizens. There are a large number of amateur artists here who have developed marked talent, and specimens of their work are sold in the various stores in the city. The historic interest which centers in the old missions, together with the many romantic scenes about the city, furnish fruitful subjects for the artist, and cause a large and constantly increasing demand for their productions."[12]

An early and active art colony had taken root in the city, and it included some of the state's most accomplished artists. In addition to Gentilz and Lungkwitz, early San Antonio artists of the period included Robert Onderdonk and Edward Grenet. Of these, the pioneer artist Onderdonk, who had moved to the city in 1879 after studying at the National Academy of Design, proved to be a singular force in advancing painting in Texas. He prolifically produced images of the region, he taught many of the important artists in San Antonio and later Dallas, and he was father to a later generation of prominent Texas artists. In 1887, Onderdonk helped to establish San Antonio's first art organization, the Van Dyke Art Club, and this group held important art exhibitions for its members beginning in that year.[13]

Art was also beginning to take root in other parts of the state as well. Texas had begun to include annual art exhibitions at its state fairs as early as 1886. By 1893, Robert Onderdonk had moved from San Antonio to Dallas and there established the Dallas Art Students' League.[14] In making the move, Onderdonk was hoping that wealthy Dallasites would be more generous in their support of local artists than had the social elite of San Antonio, whose newly acquired artistic tastes had been more given to European work or that of more established American artists.[15] Beginning in the late 1870s, the state of Texas gave a boost to indigenous painters through commissions for portraits of Texas patriots and early governors, as well as for his-

torical scenes that related the birth of the Republic. About this same time, colleges and universities began to spring up within the state, serving to attract additional working artists to Texas as well as affording more opportunities for interested art students. Increased urbanization and expanded educational opportunities within the state gave rise to colonies of artists, which formed in Houston, Dallas, El Paso, Austin, San Antonio, and elsewhere.

The cause was also aided by the formation of the Texas Federation of Women's Clubs in 1897. This group provided a wonderful infrastructure of prominent women who advocated study and appreciation of the arts. The Texas Fine Arts Association was founded in 1911, and it provided strong advocacy for the arts by petitioning the state legislature to appoint the Texas Commission for the Arts. Additionally this association promoted art education in the state's public schools and created an endowed chair at the University of Texas devoted to teaching the history, principles, and appreciation of art. Furthermore, the Texas Fine Arts Association organized the first exhibit of Texas artists outside the state, orchestrating an exhibition at Nashville, Tennessee, in 1927.[16] This association and the state Federation of Women's Clubs were instrumental in founding a series of local art leagues and associations. So successful were they that by 1928 William J. Battle reported active art organizations in Austin, Dallas, Waco, Fort Worth, Galveston, Houston, San Antonio, and Abilene.[17] However, in his 1926 article entitled "Art in the Southwest," Marion Murray reminds us that such local activity was not confined to the larger cities, stating that "literally from El Paso to Texarkana various Texas towns, guided by energetic committees, have arranged exhibits, heard lectures and made an intelligent effort to learn."[18] These leagues begot local art schools, and these, in turn, supported numerous artist camps about the state.

The artist camps were usually active in the spring and summer and featured sketching or painting lessons in the field under the tutelage of prominent artists and/or instructors of the day. They also offered participating artists opportunities for varied subjects, camaraderie, and travel throughout the state. Some of the most popular were organized by Frank Reaugh, including sketching trips to Palo Duro Canyon. Other artists, such as Alexandre Hogue and Emma Richardson Cherry, organized popular field courses in remote and scenic spots, such as Glen Rose or the Texas coast. One of the largest and most successful of these artist camps was established at Christoval, a few miles outside of San Angelo. This camp was organized in 1921 by Mollie L. Crowther, and it ran each summer until her death in 1927. It was a popular camp for Texas artists and counted among its teaching faculty many of the state's most prominent artists of the period, including José Arpa, Rolla Taylor, Olin Travis, and Xavier Gonzalez.[19]

While art schools and artist camps provided an important communications network for practicing artists, the general public's art interests were heightened by increased coverage in the Texas news media. Whether they led the way, or were simply pulled along by growing public interest, Texas newspapers must be given some credit for promoting the arts at the turn of the century. Through their publicity of local art events and their inclusion of regular columns and features extolling the virtues of local artists, the press contrib-

uted to the state's growing appreciation for the arts. Scholarly epithets on the arts also began to appear in the newly established art departments at state universities. The *Southwest Review,* published at Southern Methodist University in Dallas, became the state's first literary journal to devote serious attention to issues of regional art, providing a "forum for aesthetic and philosophical discussions for both literary and visual arts within the Southwest."[20]

Finally, such museums as the Witte, majestic permanent domiciles for the display and study of art, became a part of the Texas landscape. These facilities were natural projects of locally active art leagues and greatly contributed to the public's increased interest during this era. Leading the way was the Fort Worth Library and Art Gallery chartered in 1892 by twenty-four women in that city.[21] Houston, Dallas, and of course, San Antonio followed, and all of these cities had developed museums by the latter half of the twenties.

These forces all combined to bring new artists to the fore in a state where artistic talent had heretofore been sparse. With a rise in the number of artists working in Texas came a concomitant elevation in the standards of accomplishment among these artists. By 1926, Texas could boast that four members of its indigenous art community had exhibited with the National Academy of Design. Frank Reaugh, Edward G. Eisenlohr, and the young Reveau Bassett, all of Dallas, were included in exhibitions at the time. San Antonio's contribution to the prestigious academy was Julian Onderdonk, the son of Robert, whose death in 1922 was an untimely and serious loss to the state's emergent art fortunes.[22]

The Davis competitions, then, came at a critical

juncture in the state's art history. It was an opportune time for an event of this subject and magnitude, as the 1920s and the preceding decade had turned out to be watershed years for painting in Texas. This era has been aptly described by Fisk as a time of a "quickening of the arts in Texas."[23] In selecting this particular venue for their art patronage, both Davis and the San Antonio Art League were acutely aware of the dynamic growth of the arts in Texas. They certainly must have sensed the state's emerging position in the arts and recognized the important cultural contributions of such a contest.

Perhaps Davis and his art league colleagues were also cognizant of a growing regional genre among artists working in the state at that time. Certainly, as more and more Texas artists undertook more and more Texas subjects, with the distinctive forms and colors of the area, a regionalist tradition was bound to take shape. Even before 1920, for instance, the bluebonnet was already established as a popular subject in Texas art, with such leading artists as Nannie Huddle, Janet Downie, and José Arpa executing many excellent examples. Certainly Julian Onderdonk had already attained a national reputation by this time as the genius of this particular floral subject and had painted what is now recognized as the masterpiece of this genre in 1922 with his *Dawn in the Hills*.[24] By the 1920s the bluebonnet motif had been expanded to include a broader range of indigenous subjects. In his 1928 article in *Southwest Review*, W. J. Battle, of the University of Texas, listed the "joy of painting ranch life, Texas landmarks, Texas flowers and the Texas character" as distinctive homegrown subjects that sustained most of the state's artists, keeping them happily at work in the Lone Star State instead

of plying their talents elsewhere.[25] Dallas's Edward Eisenlohr expressed strong agreement on the abundance of opportunities that existed for Texas painters when he stated that "if you can't find a landscape worth painting within ten miles of where you are, then you shouldn't be a painter. There is much to paint here. Dallas sits waiting for her artists to put her on canvas."[26] Indeed it was the Dallas art colony that became the most vocal in the late 1920s with regard to creating a coherent regional expression and style. In sponsoring an art contest that focused on Texas scenes, Edgar Davis emphasized that he was fulfilling his own personal, mystical obligation to the flora of his newly adopted state. In actuality, by selecting Texas wildflowers, ranch life, and cotton farming as subjects for his competitions, he was reinforcing, deliberately or otherwise, a growing regional aesthetic that was important to Texas art at the time.

Although not an intended outcome, the Davis competitions also helped to introduce the debate over modern art trends in Texas. Texas' artistic evolution had coincided with the progressive art movements that were played out in their various forms between 1890 and 1930, frequently creating a maelstrom of controversy in the art centers of Europe and America's East Coast. In 1926, when the San Antonio Art League launched the wildflower competitions, there were few Texas artists who could be called avant-garde. Romantic realism enjoyed great popular acceptance, and many artists in the state experimented with impressionist methods as a vehicle for their realistic tendencies. Most of the American artists entering the Davis contests were trained in the academies of New York and Paris, and certainly the contest judges reflected this background.[27] However, a growing number of the younger artists entering the competitions were influenced by modern art trends and had already begun to reject impressionism as a mode for conveying their unique Texas subjects. Many began to experiment with a stylistic approach more akin to what would later be called "American Scene." While some of this modern art was selected for exhibition in the Davis competitions, the contest judges consistently demonstrated a conspicuous preference for the more conservative academic renderings in their award of prizes. Naturally, the redeeming qualities of conservative versus modern art became a point of contention among some. The fact that this concern would arise in conjunction with these contests is illustrative of the maturation and the growing diversification of the art community in Texas at the time. The events provided one of the first forums in the state for these issues to be debated. Thus, while the Davis competitions became something of a lightning rod for young Texas modernists, such as Alexandre Hogue or Jerry Bywaters, the contests actually helped to define one of the more important tenets of the vigorous Texas regionalist school of the thirties—a strong rejection of impressionism.

So it was within this time and milieu that the idea of the Texas Wildflower Competitive Exhibitions was born. These were unprecedented art events for the state and proved to be extremely significant for the fledgling Texas art scene. Through the competitions, Edgar Davis was at long last supplying the needed "commissions," which were necessary to entice the country to paint Texas and which the railroads and government had earlier failed to provide. And since scalping had long since fallen from favor, the state was ripe for

art and the Texas regional aesthetic was set to flourish.

To gain a full measure of appreciation for the Davis competitions, however, one must understand the patron of these events. He first arrived in Texas, already well established as a businessman, a few years after World War I. He had previously amassed an early fortune in the shoe manufacturing business and had added to that largesse by establishing America's pioneering rubber plantations in Sumatra in the early years of the century. His work in the rubber industry had established him as one of the nation's corporate giants, as he became a major stockholder and served as a member of the board of directors of the United States Rubber Company for almost a decade.

Davis's introduction to Texas, and to Luling in particular, came as a result of his investigation of oil play in the vicinity on behalf of his brother, who had invested in stock in one of the area's earliest drilling operations. Sensing a destiny of purpose, and assessing the prospects as favorable, he proceeded to assume his brother's interests and almost immediately began to drill for oil on his own in the Austin chalk formations of the surrounding area. Although unsuccessful at first, his persistence enabled him to develop the Luling field, the interests in which he sold to Magnolia Oil in 1926 for $12,100,000, the single largest financial transaction in the Texas oil industry to that time.[28]

This success as a wildcatter, coupled with his earlier entrepreneurial exploits, would have been sufficient to establish Davis's place in the legacy of the Texas oil industry, but it was his penchant for giving away his money that set him apart in a state brimming with successful oil magnates. In addition to his business prowess, Edgar Davis was also a man of deep faith and mystical conviction. He believed that his financial successes were the direct result of divine intervention and envisioned himself as a vessel for the transfer of his considerable material wealth to the public good. Thus, after his windfall from the Magnolia sale, Davis wasted little time in sharing his wealth. Among his many philanthropic gestures, he invested heavily in the arts, including his underwriting the Texas Wildflower Competitive Exhibitions.

It is said that Davis's affinity for Texas wildflowers traced back to his earliest and least successful days as a wildcatter in Luling, at which time his spirits were sustained by the brilliant fields of flowers that blanketed the Texas hillsides. Ostensibly, his feelings for the native flora were so strong that he was compelled to underwrite this exhibition of wildflower paintings in hopes that it might convey to others the beauty and hope that he had experienced in his times of challenge. Thus in the three years of the competitions, Davis awarded over $53,000 in prize money for paint-ings of Texas wildflowers, ranch life, and cotton farming. In addition, he spent large sums on galas and related social functions to promote the exhibitions and to entertain participating artists and patrons.

Edgar B. Davis was truly the ideal patron for the Texas Wildflower Competitive Exhibitions, and his mystical vision and philosophy of faith are clearly manifested in these historical episodes. His full exploits are seemingly larger than life and his story only begins with the brief synopsis above. Wilbur Matthews, the San Antonio attorney who defended Davis in many of his legal wrangles, summed it up perfectly when he wrote that "an imaginative novelist could not create a fictitious character to compare with the real Edgar B. Davis."[29] What follows, therefore, is the intriguing story of one of the state's long forgotten but true-to-life characters, Edgar B. Davis, and the rich art legacy he left us through the Texas Wildflower Competitive Exhibitions.

CHAPTER TWO

A Man of Faith
and a Man of Vision

Edgar Byrum Davis was born on February 2, 1873, in what is now Brockton, Massachusetts. He was the youngest of five children born to Stephen and Julia (Copeland) Davis. Both parents had roots deep in Massachusetts, tracing back to the earliest Pilgrims.[1] In rearing the young Edgar and his siblings, Stephen and Julia reflected the puritanical values of their famous forebears, who had come to America in search of religious freedom and had endured many hardships in the course of their settlement. Indeed, many of those Pilgrim virtues, such as unconventional religious beliefs, hard work, and uncommon perseverance in the face of hardship, proved to be defining characteristics of the young Edgar's persona and unquestionably influenced his remarkable achievements in later years.

Stephen Davis, a veteran of the Civil War, was a shoe cutter by trade. Julia was a devoted homemaker, whose deep religious convictions profoundly influenced Edgar. By Edgar's birth, Stephen had developed a small but successful shoe manufacturing concern; however,

his entrepreneurial successes were short-lived, as the business fell prey to the depression of 1875. Undaunted, Stephen remained in the shoe manufacturing business, joining the George Kieth Company. Thus, while work was consistent for Stephen, income was modest for the Davis household during Edgar's formative years. One must infer, however, that the father's work was well regarded, as the shoe company, now called Kieth's Walkover Shoe Company, later employed his eldest son, Oscar, who likewise served that company with distinction, ultimately earning positions as a board member and officer of the firm.[2]

Edgar meanwhile entered Huntington Grammar School in Brockton, and completed his formal education with his graduation from Brockton High School in 1889. Although he had a strong desire to go to Harvard University to continue his education and to play football, Edgar was unable to attend college due to the limited finances of the family. Athletic scholarships, of course, were unheard of in those days, so Edgar's dream of playing end at Harvard was unfulfilled—a lasting regret until his dying day. Had not finances precluded his participation in college football, his size alone might have made his athletic career a great success. Upon his graduation from high school, Edgar touched the mark of 6'4" tall and weighed in at well above 250 pounds, a veritable giant in his era. In addition to his ample proportions, the young Davis had also displayed considerable athleticism in his play on the line for Brockton High School and other local community teams. While the dream of college football eluded him, Davis did develop a lifelong passion for sports and, in later years, frequented many sporting events in conjunction with his travels about the country.[3]

Upon graduation from high school, Edgar tried his hand briefly as a newspaper reporter, followed by experimentation with a number of other jobs. Inevitably, however, he soon followed in the footsteps of his father, and by now his older brother Oscar, when he began work in Brockton with Isaac Emerson, a local shoemaker. He went next to the Eaton and Terry Company, another local shoe manufacturing concern, and when the Charles A. Eaton Company was spun off in 1893, Edgar Davis was employed as a bookkeeper and awarded a five percent interest in the firm. It was at Eaton that the young Davis first displayed his natural instincts for business, his propensity for hard work, and his devotion to corporate success. Beginning first as a bookkeeper, he soon worked his way up within the company to the position of treasurer and later sales manager, with twenty-five percent ownership in the business. In his capacity as sales manager for the Eaton company, Davis is credited with introducing national advertising to the shoe industry, going so far as em-

bossing the likeness of Charles Eaton on the sole of each pair of shoes.[4] It was also during this time that Edgar Davis began the first of his extensive international travels, touring Europe at the turn of the century on a combination business-travel excursion.[5]

Events changed suddenly and dramatically for Edgar Davis beginning in 1904. First, Davis suffered what he perceived to be a serious career setback when Charles Eaton promoted his own son into a position that Edgar perceived to be rightfully his. Davis was deeply disappointed by Eaton's actions and resolved to leave the firm and divest himself of his ownership position in the business. Although profoundly troubling to him at the time, this episode proved instrumental in the young Davis's future prospects in two important ways. First, the career "setback" actually netted Davis his first fortune, as the sale of his Eaton interests yielded the young man, barely thirty years of age at the time, a tidy sum in excess of $1,000,000.[6] Additionally, this incident fostered a lifelong devotion to fairness, equity, and charity toward his employees, principles that Davis consistently manifested in his later corporate and personal affairs. This compassion and regard for the well-being of his employees, coupled with his genuine willingness to share the economic success of the corporation, became central to Davis's management philosophy. His devout concern for and generosity to those who worked for him set him dramatically apart from the conventional captains of American industry in the early years of this century.

His troubles at the Eaton firm were accentuated when he experienced an unusual mystical phenomenon late in 1904. In his autobiographical account of 1949, Davis recounted his experience: "Something happened in my life on December 1, 1904, which led me to believe that I had a Mission in Life, and I want to record the great Results which have come through my life of Faith in God which I have lived—very weakly at times I fear—ever since."[7]

Although the circumstances remain obscure, Davis confided in later years to a number of intimates what he actually encountered on that December day in 1904. He explained that he was told by "The Voice" of a high mission, including the revelation that he was "Called of God to be President of the United States." In later years, Davis would never speak these words aloud but would instead write them on a sheet of paper, share them with his confidant, and immediately burn them after being read. Apparently he proceeded with this ritual on several occasions and kept a list of his enlightened friends in his safe deposit box.[8]

The years immediately following his departure from Eaton were dark and troubling for Davis, though a wealthy young man. He remained deeply despondent about the events that had caused him to be overlooked for promotion. In addition, Edgar's continuing efforts to come to grips with the mysterious and profound December message seriously affected his emotional well-being. At last, the years of prolonged work with Eaton, coupled with his severe emotional stress, gave way to depression, and in 1904 Davis suffered a series of mental breakdowns. In his later writings Davis referred to these breakdowns and hospitalizations, stating that he "suffered greatly thereby." These emotional disorders occurred almost immediately after his mystical encounter. He reported that "these hospitalizations left me with melancholia which I had great difficulty in overcoming for a number of years."[9] He later de-

scribed this time in a letter to friends as one of the "hard experiences of life" and referred to his condition at the time as a "fit of insanity . . . from which I suffered the torments of the damned."[10]

January of 1907 found Davis in improved condition but apparently still locked in a struggle to regain the full measure of his emotional health. At this time he was encouraged by his physician to undertake an extended overseas voyage ostensibly for health purposes. What followed was an adventure that not only aided in restoring Davis's health but also opened, almost providentially, the next chapter in the entrepreneur's remarkable business career.

It was during this recuperative voyage that Davis first discovered the enormous profits garnered by Dutch and British rubber plantations. In making this discovery, it seems that the Fates intervened as they seemed to do so often for Edgar Davis in his roller-coaster career. For he was poised to return home after a stop in Cairo but changed his itinerary at the last minute. He extended his tour for another trip around half of the world in order to accommodate an old acquaintance (and unbeknownst to him at the time, a future business partner), Walter Mahoney, who had become ill during the trip.[11] At subsequent stops in Malaya and Sumatra, the young tourists observed the large rubber plantations in the area. Davis, ever the businessman, was intrigued by the possibilities and applied himself to learning as much as he could about the cultivation, manufacture, and marketing of rubber. His research convinced him of the profitability of cultivated rubber, and it also became apparent to him that a stable and dependable American supplier was necessary to support the country's emerging automobile industry. These investigations proved to be of great interest and importance to Davis and prompted his decision to pursue American development of cultivated rubber. Thus, his chance introduction to the growth of rubber not only opened the door for his next great financial exploits but initiated a lifelong interest and devotion.

Edgar Davis returned from his cruise in 1908, apparently sound enough in mind and body to try to make a go of a new shoe manufacturing enterprise. Edgar's new concern was financed in part by his brother, Oscar, since the years of respite and medical expenses had depleted his fortune. Still, Edgar could not dispel his newfound interest in cultivated rubber and remained convinced of the enormous profits and economic benefits that would accrue to the U.S. corporation that

Edgar B. Davis in Sumatra, ca. 1915. Davis (center) *is shown with associate Louis Leibowitz and a trusted elephant trainer. Davis implemented state-of-the-art farming techniques in his rubber plantations to achieve high profits for the United States Rubber Company. A devout Christian, Davis kept the Sabbath; likewise, he noted that the elephants also refused to work on Sundays. Courtesy Riley Froh Collection*

first secured its own stable source of crude rubber. On holiday with his older brother at a retreat in upstate New York, the younger Davis met John J. Watson, a vice president of the United States Rubber Company.[12] Through this encounter, Edgar Davis was eventually able to secure an audience with officials of U.S. Rubber to present his plans for American-operated rubber plantations in the Far East. It speaks volumes of Davis's business acumen when one considers the backdrop of his negotiations with U.S. Rubber. Here was a young shoe man, still in his middle thirties, his early fortune seriously depleted due to his medical expenses in recovering from an emotional illness. He possessed absolutely no prior experience in the rubber industry and actually had no experience in cultivating any crop, much less rubber. Despite these obvious shortcomings, he had somehow gained access to the board of the most powerful rubber company in the world, and now stood poised to convince them to invest several million dollars of corporate funds to establish plantations half a world away, and to place *him* in charge of these operations. A lesser man might have found the prospects daunting, but somehow, as though guided by Providence, Edgar Davis was successful in gaining the company's support. He secured a pledge of $1,500,000 for start-up operations. Although the United States Rubber Company initially provided Davis with only about ten percent of the capital that he had requested for the operations of the plantations, he was able to arrange the additional finances himself. In 1910 he acquired some 90,000 acres for U.S. Rubber in Sumatra.[13] In that year, he personally oversaw planting of the first rubber trees for cultivation. These became the first

American rubber plantations and, under the supervision of the novice Davis, these vast farms were highly productive, with yields per acre far exceeding other established plantations in the area. The innovative management techniques introduced by Davis and his staff were soon emulated by competing British and Dutch concerns.

He also negotiated a profitable arrangement for himself, acquiring an annual salary of $12,000, plus expenses, as well as an 8.7 percent commission on the value of the plantations after full productivity.[14] True to his projections, the plantations did prove to be a source of substantial profits for the giant rubber concern and were roundly credited with maintaining the financial solvency of the United States Rubber Company in the years immediately following World War I, when rubber prices fluctuated wildly. In their 1936 book, *Rubber: A Story of Glory and Greed,* Howard and Ralph Wolf characterize the plantations as "the best investment the one-time rubber trust ever made, and by far its single most important asset."[15] Given the success and strategic importance of the plantations, Davis was rewarded with a place on the board of directors. He served as financial officer for the board and was twice offered the presidency of the corporation, which he declined.[16]

While in the employ of U.S. Rubber, Edgar Davis digressed from the business of business long enough to contribute his management prowess to the American cause during World War I. Confident in his vision and calling for national leadership, he, along with his young assistant, David Figart, took it upon himself to shape and promote a plan for the strategic bombing of the German transportation system. Davis corresponded with President Woodrow Wilson and even gained audiences with members of the Wilson cabinet as well as several influential War Department officials to convince them of the merits of his plan.[17] He even weathered a stormy encounter with Theodore Roosevelt, the old Rough Rider himself, in an attempt to leverage the former president's support for his approach.[18] The First World War ended, however, before Davis had achieved any serious commitment to his initiatives. Later, in World War II, Davis would resurrect this plan and again aggressively market the strategy through his influential friends and associates. This time, though, the Allies would indeed employ a bombing strategy remarkably similar to Davis's, eventually crippling German military movements and preparedness. While Davis received no credit for this success, there is some evidence to suggest that the genesis of the Allied tactics in World War II were the original Davis documents that had resurfaced from War Department files of the First World War.[19] There can be no question that Edgar Davis was a loyal and devoted patriot. He passionately believed in the sanctity of world order and peace, and his efforts during wartime were sincerely directed toward this aim. Might, however, these civilian overtures to win the war have been a part of the man's overall strategy to achieve his own calling to the nation's highest office?

In 1919, well after the conclusion of war, and almost a decade after his unusual entrance into the rubber business, Edgar Davis resigned from the board of the United States Rubber Company. At that time he held some 60,000 shares of U.S. Rubber stock, making him the largest stockholder in the corporation. He also cashed in his reserves from the rubber plantations for a sum reported at different times between $1,800,000 and $3,500,000.[20]

Thus, in 1919, Edgar Davis's brilliant career was once again in rapid ascent. He had regained his physical and emotional health. Through his work with U.S. Rubber, he had successfully secured a second fortune, achieved much like the first, through a combination of financial savvy, salesmanship, very hard work, and—least of all—good fortune. His achievements with U.S. Rubber, coupled with his financial largesse, now made Edgar B. Davis a notable among captains of American industry. Thus endowed with corporate notoriety and sufficient resources to rank with the prominent and well-to-do, Davis became a business consultant, establishing an office at 527 Fifth Avenue in New York City. His offices there were frequented by some of America's most important capitalists, including Harvey Firestone, Cyrus Eaton, Bernard Baruch, and others.[21] Given his stock holdings in U.S. Rubber, he remained an active and prominent player in the international rubber industry. He also developed interests in automobile design and manufacturing. Davis invested in the design of a patented air-cooled engine and a novel spring suspension system in conjunction with William T. Cameron of the Cameron Car Company.[22] In late 1919, backed by Otto Kahn of Kuhn, Loeb, and Company, Davis went to Detroit with an offer to purchase Henry Ford's majority in the Ford firm. In personal correspondence later in his life, Davis would assess Ford's decline of his offer as "fortunate . . . for the automobile industry and the country."[23] During his business consulting days, Davis once again meddled in presidential affairs, publishing a pamphlet entitled *The Big Business of Government,* which recommended that the president's cabinet be restructured to four members, each overseeing several departments. The report was seriously debated by at least one congressional committee.[24]

Immediately after his resignation from U.S. Rubber, Davis displayed his personal inclination to share benefits with employees and friends. As a board member for U.S. Rubber, he had advocated a profit-sharing plan for employees, a progressive idea for its time, and one that did not gain corporate acceptance during his tenure with the corporation.[25] However, upon taking his own personal profits from the plantations in 1919, Davis did indeed "share the wealth." Invoking the earlier vows he had made in the aftermath of his disappointing Eaton experiences, Davis shared handsomely with those colleagues whose support contributed to his financial success. He gave six-figure bonuses to key assistants and followed with gifts of decreasing amounts to staff, secretaries, maids, and other attendants at his hotel residence in New York City. So generous was Davis in rewarding these workers that, in all, he gave gifts equal to almost two-thirds of his total U.S. Rubber settlement. At one point in this spree of postprofit distribution, Edgar, apparently moved by the spirit of giving, confided in his brother Oscar that it was his "hope to die a poor man." To which Oscar retorted cleverly, "at the rate you are going, you will almost certainly get your wish."[26]

Thus, for perhaps the first time, Edgar B. Davis was able to bring to life his management philosophy of sharing corporate success with employees. Based upon the writings and actions of his later career there can be no doubt that he was sincerely committed to this tenet. In 1920, he published a brochure entitled *The Dawn of a New Day: Containing Suggestions for the Introduction of a New Industrial Order.* In this pamphlet, which predates the New Deal by almost ten years, Davis went on record in the corporate community for giving workers the opportunity to buy stock. He further promoted the establishment of what he called an American Cooperative Association, dedicated to assuring the interests of "justice to labor." Finally, he requested that Congress establish and appoint an Industrial Relations Commission with the intended purpose and authority to "hear and evaluate all facts bearing on the division of surplus profits between Capital, Labor and Management and recommend fair bases for distribution."[27] In later years, he would revisit this theme in a 1932 article in the *North American Review* entitled "The Way Out— And On." In this particular writing, he opined that "the most urgent need today in the rehabilitation of business is that it should be done at ample profit, with generous distributions made to workers, management and shareholders."[28]

In the article, he went further to declare that "workers on farm, in mine and in factory and in all other walks of life must share in this business-profit motive. The permanent prosperity of manufacturer, shareholder, merchant, capitalist and the general public is dependent upon the economic security of the workers and the safety of their investments."[29]

Behind the scenes of his corporate success, Davis continued to contemplate the mission that he believed God had handed him through his mysterious encounter in 1904. He maintained an interest in mysticism, religion, and philosophy. He became an avid reader and a devoted student in these areas. His experiences in Sumatra, coupled with extensive travel in the region, introduced him to religious thought of the East. Through this, he became deeply interested in the concept of reincarnation and ideas related to transmigration of the soul. As his religious views broadened, he also refined the personal ideology that guided his daily transactions and that he later came to call "practical Christianity."[30] Likewise, his interpretation of his mission assumed greater dimension. He came to believe that his access to wealth was a result of divine intervention and that his purpose was to serve as a conduit for the transfer of this material wealth to the public good. These images were vivid to Davis and thus became the basis of his every action in life and in business.

In the ensuing years, he acquired even greater wealth, which he continued to share generously with community, friends, and colleagues—achieving, at times, a reputation for eccentricity in dispersing his hard-earned fortunes. His genuine belief that God would guide him in pursuit of his mission enabled him to pursue ventures with a faith and confidence that often defied conventional wisdom and technical expertise of the day. He took what appeared to be dramatic risks in his business pursuits, all the while confident that he was being counseled and guided by a higher authority and with a higher purpose in mind. This facet of Davis's persona cannot be underestimated and contributes to his status as one of the remarkable personalities of his day. His many entrepreneurial accomplishments and social contributions may all in some way be traced to his mysterious encounter and the consequent vision of stewardship and applied Christianity he attained.

He continued to believe that the mission would lead him, at some point, to the presidency of the United States. Exactly how he envisioned achieving this position is not known, for Edgar Davis had an aversion for publicity and self-promotion, seldom granting interviews and audiences with the press. He eschewed campaigning and must have determined that his works alone would bring him sufficient acclaim so as to render campaigning for the presidency an unnecessary step. Apparently he envisioned that he would be drafted by popular opinion into the nation's chief executive role. In 1927, he was, in fact, mentioned as an early candidate for the vice presidency prior to the Democratic convention, a move promoted by significant political operatives in both Massachusetts and Texas. Davis received overtures from several influential figures, including the governor of Massachusetts, in attempts to seriously advance his candidacy for the vice presidency. He was, however, slow to respond and gave only tacit support to these efforts on his behalf. As a result, his campaign never really got off the ground and he was granted only a complimentary nomination for the position on the convention floor.[31] Nonetheless, he apparently continued to aspire to the presidency. He reflected upon the nature of a Davis White House as late as 1932, in statements recorded by his assistant in May of that year. In these notes, Davis offered the following political insights: "There will be no back doors to the White House when I get there. I will recognize neither friend nor foe. Popularity is fickle. The thing to do is to play the game and carry the people with you."[32]

Oddly, however, in similar notes made by his secretary only a few days later, Davis proclaimed the presidency to be his "stumbling block." The notes offer further elaboration of this statement: "How could I believe this? The effort to do so drove me insane. But I believe that my mission has to do with world peace."[33]

While we cannot discern Davis's true feelings with regard to the presidency, we may conclude from the above reference that he approached the position with some trepidation, as it had been in his past a source of great personal turmoil and strife. Perhaps this offers some insight into Davis's personal reticence to politick actively for the office. Nevertheless he again revealed his interests in the nation's chief executive role in correspondence of August, 1932, directed to David Figart. At the time of this letter Davis was enthusiastically awaiting the development of his oil properties in the Buckeye field, which he believed to be of immense value. He also believed that this discovery and its disposition held the key to addressing his financial woes at the time, as well as the key to fulfilling what he believed to be his God-given mission. To Figart he wrote, "This may sound crazy to you but I know something of the power that is back of me. I think—I do not know—that not only will Buckeye come in time to permit me to meet all my obligations, but that it will be of such size that the whole oil industry will take notice. We will sell all or part to advantage; that it will bring me into national prominence and that there will be a citizen's movement (in which I will not lift a finger) for me to run as independent THIS YEAR" (Davis's emphasis).[34]

Notwithstanding Davis's own personal view of the presidency, there is some evidence to show that others did recognize in him a certain potential for the position. In their treatise on the history of the rubber industry, Wolf and Wolf provided their impression "that one or the other of the great American political parties has overlooked the best bet in its history by failing to nominate him [Davis] for the Presidency."[35]

In 1919, however, it was Edgar Davis the management consultant who arrived in Luling, Texas, to investigate oil interests in the area on behalf of his brother, who was now vice president of the Kieth shoe manufacturing firm. Oscar had bought into drilling interests in Luling earlier in the year and offered Edgar a third of the profits if he agreed to manage the investment.[36] One must wonder today what impressions passed through the minds of the residents of tiny Luling the first time they observed this gentlemanly giant from New York City lumbering about their community. Davis was still straight and tall at 6'4". He had grown in girth and weighed a portly 350 pounds. He often dressed in the white suits he had come to appreciate during his exotic travels in the Far East. No doubt the new Yankee in town must have presented a curious sight, turning heads and drawing comments from Luling residents as he strode into action.

By late 1919, Davis had completed his initial investigation of Oscar's leases in the Luling area and, based on advice of his geologist, selected the first site for drilling. Their first drilling venture, the Mozelle No. 1, proved unsuccessful, essentially depleting his brother's initial $75,000 investment.[37] Upon review of the situation, Oscar Davis determined to cut his losses and refrain from further investment. He turned over his complete interests to Edgar, who accepted with the intention of repaying his brother at the time of his strike.

Davis immediately directed the drilling of a second well, the Thompson No. 1, which also proved to be a dry hole. In the course of drilling the Thompson well, Davis invested heavily of his own resources, spending in excess of $65,000 through 1920.[38] With two wells down at substantial loss, and having exhausted the original investment of his brother, Davis decided to continue drilling in the area, but this time to go it on his own. In 1921, he formed the United North and South Oil Company and assumed the presidency of the corporation. Typical of his philosophy of reconciliation, Davis selected the name of his company "because he thought it might show some easing of the strain which he still found between Yankees and Rebels" in 1920 Texas.[39]

Under the auspices of United North and South, Davis drilled again. This well, the Cartwright No. 1, also proved fallow. He authorized Cartwright No. 2, yielding yet another disappointment. Cartwright No. 3 and Ghormley wells were yet additional dusters.

Finally, on his seventh try, and only after having to remove his drilling equipment due to a title problem, did Edgar Davis find oil. Not much at first, but in the Rafael Rios No. 1, Davis did secure a marginal producer, bolstering his confidence as well as the flagging resources of his company.[40]

No doubt, the Rios No. 1 had come to Davis just in the nick of time. After six consecutive dry holes, and a number of other investment shortfalls, Davis's personal fortune was—once again—all but gone. He was heavily indebted to local banks and merchants and frequently unable to meet payroll demands. On one occasion, it was necessary for him to sell his automobile and his New York office furniture in order to gain transport to his drilling sites in Texas. At his lowest point Davis could not even secure the $285 necessary

Edgar B. Davis of Luling, Texas, ca. 1930. Here Davis is shown in the prime of his oil days, flush with the resources of his Luling oil discovery and subsequent sale to Magnolia. In these days, Davis was an imposing figure, carrying over three hundred pounds on his 6'4" frame. Courtesy Genealogical and Historical Society of Caldwell County

to insure his drilling operations. Grasping at straws, he recalled $300 in British war bonds back in his safe in Brockton and immediately wired his secretary to cash them in. To his surprise, she located an additional $80,000 in British war bonds that Davis had forgotten. He took this as an omen to continue drilling, and with this money, and a $4,000 mortgage on his pumping equipment, he sustained his operations for several more weeks.[41] Thus, the Rios well was critical for Davis but certainly was not sufficient to relieve him of his now substantial financial burdens.

What an amazing reversal of fortune this must have seemed to his friends and colleagues, and perhaps even to Edgar Davis himself. He had arrived in small, dusty Luling, Texas, a wealthy industrialist and respected veteran of the corporate boardrooms of the East. In a matter of just over two years, he had sunk his personal fortune into a series of dry Texas holes. Now, instead of a comfortable endowment, Davis had only a marginal test well, producing a meager 150 barrels of oil a day and, as of yet, no defined field. Driven by his vision, he was compelled to drill more, and this in the face of considerable professional discouragement. Edgar Davis was advised repeatedly by geologists to abandon drilling in the Luling area, with most feeling that the Edwards lime and Austin chalk formations around Luling would never produce profitable quantities of oil. The editor of the *Luling Signal* recalled a letter from a recognized geologist stating, "In an ordinary wildcat well, you have one chance in a hundred. Here in this situation, you have but a fraction of one percent of a chance."[42]

Secured by his faith and his tendency to pursue his ends in the face of insurmountable odds, Davis continued to drill, somehow certain that vast reserves lay below the rugged terrain of Caldwell County. After the Rafael Rios discovery well on August 9, 1921, Davis continued with his severe cash struggle until the middle of 1922 when, at last, upon his inspection of the Merriweather well, he was immersed in the black goodness of a gusher.[43]

This magnificent well enabled Davis to attract the necessary funds to drill more aggressively, and thus to map out successfully the parameters of the Luling field. By the end of 1923, the rubber magnate turned wildcatter had secured eight more producers, and Luling's boom was well underway. The years after 1923 were prosperous and busy ones for Davis. He continued successful exploration and development in the Luling

Edgar Davis in silhouette. This interesting photograph of the entrepreneur in middle age projects the profile of a refined and worldly gentleman. The artistry of this particular photograph is illustrative of Davis's intrigue with the visual arts, paintings, and photography. Courtesy Genealogical and Historical Society of Caldwell County

field and in adjacent areas. By 1924 no one could doubt that Edgar B. Davis had succeeded as a wildcatter in the Texas oil business. Repeating his experiences in the rubber enterprise, he had once more entered a field with virtually no firsthand experience and had come out ahead. Once again, Edgar Davis had parlayed good fortune and tenacity into bountiful success, and this time, all was done in the face of conventional wisdom and the professional expertise of the era. In late 1926, Edgar Davis sold his interests in the Luling field to Magnolia Oil, the forerunner of Mobil Oil Corporation, for $12,100,000, the single largest transaction in

the Texas oil industry to that date. He took half of the price in cash and the other half in installments paid out of future production. He retained rights to all oil below 3,000 feet on his leases in the Luling field.[44]

Consistent with his vision, Edgar Davis had once again become the instrument of great wealth. Having already secured fortunes in the shoe business and the rubber industry, Davis was truly wealthy and widely regarded as something of an entrepreneurial genius, albeit an unorthodox one.

It was, for Davis, a time to share. Almost immediately after his sale to Magnolia, Davis devised a plan

The Luling oil field, ca. 1925. After early failure, and against all advice to the contrary, Edgar Davis persisted in discovering the rich Luling field. It was the wildflowers shrouding the hills of Luling that sustained his efforts in the earliest and most trying of his wildcatting days. Courtesy Genealogical and Historical Society of Caldwell County

to disperse his newfound wealth to those who had directly and indirectly contributed to his wildcatting success. He determined that he would provide cash bonuses for his management team and each employee. In addition, he envisioned projects that would enhance the quality of life for the citizens of his hometown of Brockton and adopted Texas home of Luling. On June 5, 1926, in what was certain to be one of Texas' biggest barbecues ever, Davis staged a grand celebration and announced his generous intentions. The event itself was stupendous, attracting crowds estimated at between 15,000 to 40,000 people. To accommodate the great numbers, Davis nearly bought out the merchants of Caldwell County—procuring over 12,200 pounds of beef, over 5,180 pounds of mutton, 2,000 fryers, 8,700 ice cream sandwiches, 85 gallons of ice cream, 7,000 cakes, over 6,500 bottles of "near beer," and almost 29,000 soft drinks, 7,500 cigars, and 100,000 cigarettes.[45]

Understanding the segregation that existed in the Texas of 1920, Davis arranged for two parties that would occur simultaneously—one for the white community and a second for black citizens of Caldwell County. Blacks gathered for their picnic north of town, and whites assembled on newly purchased property that Davis secured along the San Marcos River. An electric welcome sign was constructed to greet guests coming to town for the event, two polished dance floors were constructed for the occasion, and the grounds of both sites were hung with several thousand Japanese lanterns. Davis arranged for entertainment, transporting dance bands to play for both gatherings and importing three New York opera stars for a special performance.[46]

Davis chose the party as his venue to announce his plans for profit sharing and community philanthropy. For his employees, he announced bonuses of up to 100 percent of their annual earnings dependent upon the tenure of their service with United North and South. Employees who had served four or more years received the bonus of 100 percent, those with three years of service received 75 percent, graduating down to 50 percent bonuses to two-year employees, and 25 percent to those with one year of service. He also announced generous bonuses, some exceeding $250,000, to each member of his five-person management team, and they also received an expense-paid vacation trip to Davis's Massachusetts home in Buzzards Bay—"The House on the Sand." Upon arrival at the Davis mansion, each found his bonus check awaiting him at the table of their first breakfast.[47] Thus Davis announced employee bonuses of almost $2,000,000 on that day.[48]

He went further, however, to announce his intentions to provide two parks for Luling citizens, one for its white citizens and one for the black community. Davis built clubhouses and swimming facilities in both parks, as well as a golf course at the white country club. He endowed both parks with a $50,000 fund to assure proper care and maintenance.

In staging this remarkable event, Davis was actually seeking to evoke biblical images of Christ providing for the many by multiplying the meager loaves of bread and fish. At the picnic, he quoted Jesus' admonition: "For what is a man profited, if he shall gain the whole world, and lose his own soul. . . . Lay not up for yourselves treasures upon earth, where moth and rust doth corrupt, and where thieves break through and steal: But lay up for yourselves treasures in heaven."

Such acts of sharing were consistent with the Davis vision and his belief that he was to transfer his material wealth to the benefit of his fellow man. Thus, while the Luling picnic represented a familiar pattern of benevolence for Davis, it caught most of the state of Texas by surprise! In later years, Davis would report that he would never again celebrate his sharing in this manner, as he felt that the true symbolism of the day was lost in press coverage. While he had hoped to stage an event that would emulate the teachings of Christ for the public, Davis must have felt that the press coverage had reduced the event to nothing more than an ostentatious party sponsored by an eccentric millionaire. Davis was no doubt correct in assessing that his message of sharing and divine accommodation of the masses was lost in the grandeur and bravado of the celebration. The newspapers gave little or no heed to his spiritual message.

In subsequent sales, such as the Darst field, which he sold for $4,000,000, Davis shared equally generously with his employees. He gave away over $1,500,000 in bonuses on this sale alone. He chose not to offer these later bonuses in grand celebration upon reflecting on his 1926 experience and reviewing the scripture that advised, "Take heed that ye do not your alms before men, to be seen of them: otherwise ye have no reward of your father which is in Heaven. Therefore when thou doest thine alms, do not sound a trumpet before thee, as the hypocrites do in the synagogues and in the streets, that they may have glory of men."[49]

Davis's philanthropy only began at the June barbecue. Later that year he acquired 1,200 acres in Luling for $250,000 and, after planning with faculty at the A&M College, he established and endowed with $750,000 the Luling Foundation demonstration farm. Through this endeavor, Davis hoped to bring progressive farming techniques to the Luling area and to diversify the cotton-based agriculture that predominated in the area. Davis had perfected his highly profitable rubber plantation using state-of-the-art farming methods, and he was convinced that transferring new farming technology to Luling would improve the economic and social prosperity of the area. Dean Edwin J. Kyle of the Texas A&M School of Agriculture (for whom the Aggies' Kyle Field is named) was instrumental in the development of the farm and served as a longtime member of its board of directors.[50]

But Davis did not forget his roots. In 1927, he also endowed a $1,000,000 foundation in his hometown of Brockton, Massachusetts. He did this in honor of his now deceased sister and brother, Amy D. Prat and Oscar C. Davis. At the suggestion of advisors, Davis named the fund the Pilgrim Foundation.[51] Both foundations continue to this day and have contributed substantially to their respective communities since their inception. With the establishment of these two community foundations, along with his profit-sharing gifts, Edgar Davis had once again lived up to his own unique standards of sharing and generosity, and once again kept the promises he had made to himself back in his early management days after his departure from Eaton. Before it was all done, Davis had given away almost five million of the six million dollars he had received in the Magnolia sale—a remarkable display of generosity, even for a man of faith.

Davis's story by no means ends here, but for the purposes of this book, it takes a turn at this point. The years from 1926 to 1929 proved to be his most com-

The Francis Oak on the Luling Foundation farm. Davis endowed the Luling Foundation as a demonstration farm. He believed strongly in modern farming techniques and agricultural diversification for the area. Working in collaboration with Texas A&M College, the farm offered classes and maintained ongoing demonstrations of new crop production and livestock management techniques. Here, a herd of the foundation's prized cattle graze below the stately old Francis Oak on the farm grounds. Courtesy Genealogical and Historical Society of Caldwell County

fortable and profitable times. It was during this, his most prosperous period, that Edgar B. Davis afforded generous support to the arts and letters and left his profound mark upon them—including his successful promotion of the Texas Wildflower Competitive Exhibitions.

In addition to his obvious talent for business, Edgar Davis had acquired "credible artistic and intel-

lectual tastes, as well as considerable talents as a singer, composer, and pianist." Riley Froh notes that Davis's art patronage was probably a logical extension of these interests, and while his fortune lasted he continued to give "vigorous financial support to paintings, music, literature and drama."[52]

Unquestionably the most phenomenal and largest of the Davis art ventures (at least in terms of cash

Scene from The Ladder. *Edgar Davis commissioned this play on the subject of reincarnation. He underwrote its two-year venue on Broadway to the tune of almost $1,500,000. Courtesy Riley Froh Collection*

from the pole that forced him to relocate to the Alamo City in search of health in the city's warmer climate.[54] By 1926, J. Frank Davis had published hundreds of articles and short stories, which had appeared in *Red Book, Scribner's,* and *Collier's,* among others. In addition, he had published three novels, all set in Texas, and claimed two one-act plays among his credentials.

After several meetings between the two old friends, Edgar Davis commissioned J. F. Davis to write a play that dealt with the concept of reincarnation. Among Edgar Davis's mystical philosophies was a belief in transmigration of the human soul. He viewed this as a plausible and "fair" ideology since it assured that all humankind could eventually achieve their just rewards in the travels of life. He and J. Frank Davis, both biblical scholars, determined to present these ideas in a play.

With script in hand, Edgar Davis enlisted the support of Broadway insider Murdock Pemberton to produce the play. The title of the piece was derived from the poem by Josiah Gilbert Holland entitled "Gradatim," in which he writes:

> *Heaven is not reached at a single bound;*
> *But we build the ladder by which we rise*
> *From the lowly earth to the vaulted skies,*
> *And we mount to its summit round by round.*[55]

The story, which traced a group of characters through four settings over a six hundred–year period, opened in late October of 1926.[56] Despite its impressive sets and well-established actors, the play was an immediate critical disaster. Davis was undaunted by the criticism of the New York press and, mustering

outlay) was his support of the Broadway play *The Ladder.* While in San Antonio in 1925, Davis chanced to meet one of his old Brockton classmates, J. Frank Davis (no relation), a former journalist who had retired to that city and was supporting himself as a freelance writer. J. F. Davis was an interesting character who had covered among his news assignment Admiral Peary's return from the North Pole and the Russo-Japanese Peace Conference.[53] In fact, it was an injury he sustained at Battle Harbor while awaiting Peary's return his usual business tenacity, vowed to make the play a success. He bolstered the flagging morale of the staff by hosting frequent stage parties. He arranged for re-writes of the play to enliven the script, employing through Pemberton some of New York's and London's most prominent playwrights to doctor the dialogue. He engaged advertising firms to hawk the play, devised promotional essay contests, and initiated a money-back guarantee for less-than-satisfied viewers. Finally, when all these strategies failed to fill the house, Davis simply gave free admission to all comers, an unheard-of prac-tice on Broadway. Despite his every effort, *The Ladder* failed to attract respectable audiences. So sparse was attendance that, during one evening performance, the husband of one of the lead actresses, seeing only a handful of patrons in the large and roomy old Cort Theater, confused the performance for a rehearsal. Director Pemberton described the amusing scene that occurred next in his article in *Esquire*, reporting that the husband "walked down the aisles of the Cort Theater leading a terrier and holding aloft a sandwich. He didn't see his wife, but saw a few people on the stage and a few in the seats. Approaching the foot-lights, he cupped his hands and shouted: 'Here's your dinner, Babs. I'm going out with the dog.' The few bewildered patrons didn't know whether this was a part of the show or not and the cast took some minutes to recover."[57]

The play proved to be a dismal failure and Davis finally withdrew it in November, 1928, over two years after its debut, but not before he issued a statement to the New York press and the city's viewing audience, explaining his reasons for support of the play. It read in part:

Scene from The Ladder. *Despite the play's lavish sets, credible cast, and unique marketing strategies, it was a critical flop and contributed to Davis's reputation for eccentricity. Courtesy Riley Froh Collection*

With a decent respect for public opinion, let me give my reasons for putting on The Ladder. *We see life about us full of suffering, seeming inequalities, and injustices. When we accept the statements of scientists that the universe has been millions of years in the making it seems to me that this brief span of threescore years and ten cannot be God's best plan for the world, but rather that our sufferings, mistakes and disappointments are but the necessary pre-cedents to our coming into harmony with a Great Plan of Life, in which we achieve our heart's desires—or something better. It was Faith in this universal success that induced me to put on* The Ladder. *It embodied no creed, it promoted no cult. The idea of reincarnation was the motif used to indicate the steps of progress toward its ultimate goal. Theater owners, players, staffs and the public have had everything to gain in our endeavor to widen the scope of the theater; but a play, like any other business, should pay its own way in order to avoid becoming a parasite on the economic body.*[58]

With this explanation, the play was soon withdrawn from New York. It went briefly to Boston for a two-week stint, and from there it was dismantled, never to be seen again. At the time that Davis "pulled the plug," *The Ladder* was the longest running play on Broadway. It also held the mark as the most expensive loss of its day, a record that presumably still stands when one accounts for inflation and other such economic gyrations. Indeed, when all expenses cleared, Edgar Davis had spent approximately $1,300,000 on the production. This expensive flop drew much attention in the popular press as an excessive waste of valuable resources. No less than Walter Winchell commented on the fiasco, concluding that Davis "would have gotten his message across better by wrapping a sandwich in a pamphlet and giving it away."[59]

Davis, however, never breathed a disparaging word about his loss, believing that the play's message had been an important one, and perhaps rationalizing a bit in his own mind that the work was ahead of its time. So steadfast were his beliefs in the message of the play that, almost twenty years later, he was still actively promoting a possible movie version of the story, presumably hoping that the medium of the motion picture and the magic of Hollywood would be able to "reincarnate" *The Ladder*.[60] The deal for the movie version was never consummated, and thus the play rests today in the archives of the Luling Historical Society.

The Ladder was by far Davis's least successful venture in the arts. He was responsible for numerous other events in the performing arts; many were noteworthy in their quality and popular acceptance. He frequently hosted concerts by New York opera figures in San Antonio and Brockton, and he staged numerous intimate performances at his two homes, "The House in the Oaks" in Luling and "The House on the Sand" in Buzzards Bay, Massachusetts. His summer concert series at the Buzzards Bay estate was especially important. He hosted twenty-one of these musical events at "The House on the Sand" from 1925 to 1929.[61] He imported leading artists from the New York Opera Society for these performances, chartering special trains for their transportation, paying their additional expenses, and of course, providing them with generous honoraria for their time. Davis had built a special studio at the Massachusetts estate, once belonging to President Grover Cleveland, expressly for such concerts.[62] The studio would accommodate approximately two hundred fifty people, and Davis was known for inviting everyone to these bayside galas, including his neighbors, domestic staff, and chauffeurs. The weekend nature of these parties frequently required that he put up many of his out-of-town patrons as guests of the estate. A 1929 newspaper account of a typical weekend concert reported that Davis housed forty-two guests and was obliged to board yet others at local hotels, assuming, of course, their expenses for their hotel stay. He advised the press at that time of his intentions to construct an annex to his Buzzards Bay estate prior to the next season that would accommodate up to eighty weekend guests.[63] The annex, however, was never built by Davis, and "The House on the Sand,"

"The House in the Oaks," Luling, Texas. Davis was forced to relinquish his beautiful home in Luling as part of a financial settlement. The home was subsequently dismantled by vandals who were never apprehended; the house was later destroyed. The site of the present-day Luling hospital is on the grounds of Davis's former home. Courtesy Genealogical and Historical Society of Caldwell County

as well as his Luling estate, would later meet sad ends.

For several seasons, Davis also imported similar troupes of Eastern performers to San Antonio and Brockton to offer concerts at Eastertime, including staging for both communities "The Last Seven Words of Christ," a cantata by Theodore Dubois.[64]

As a personal avocation, Davis also dabbled in writing his own music. He kept a piano in his home where he composed music and wrote lyrics to his songs. Given his religious devotion, his creative work was naturally given to hymns. Davis was known to perform these himself at some of his estate concerts, and his original works were also performed by certain of his guest en-

tertainers. At least two of these hymns have survived to this day, including "Christianity (The Heritage of All Mankind)" and "The Brotherhood of Man."[65]

In 1926, Edgar Davis participated in yet another important intellectual endeavor when he and his long-time partner Walter B. Mahoney acquired the *North American Review*, a venerable periodical of national importance. At the time that Davis and Mahoney acquired it, it bore the distinction of being America's oldest continuing magazine, founded in 1815. Its subscribers included prominent American scholars, businessmen, and politicians. Even Thomas Jefferson could be counted among its earliest subscribers. Contribu-

"The House on the Sand," Buzzards Bay, Massachusetts. Davis acquired his Buzzards Bay home from the estate of former president Grover Cleveland. He restored the home, adding a music conservatory. It was the site of many elaborate concerts that Davis hosted in the late 1920s, to which he transported the finest of the country's performing artists via special trains. The house and its contents were destroyed by a hurricane in 1938. Courtesy Riley Froh Collection

tors had included ten American presidents, as well as such American literary giants as Mark Twain, Lincoln Steffens, Ralph Waldo Emerson, and William Cullen Bryant. In fact, Bryant's "Thanatopsis" and Twain's "To a Person Sitting in Darkness" were first published in the *Review*. In the acquisition of the great old magazine, Davis served initially as a financial backer and later took over certain of the managerial responsibilities. He even contributed occasional articles to the publication during his term as owner. Eventually, the historical publication fell prey to the financial constraints of the Great Depression and the modern approach to literature exemplified by the emergence of *Reader's Digest*. Davis and Mahoney finally relinquished

control of the publication in 1938, selling the magazine to another publisher, who let the *Review* perish in 1940.[66]

It was also during this time of attention to the arts that Davis conceived of and endowed the Texas Wildflower Competitive Exhibitions. In 1926, Davis committed to funding the competitions, which would encourage national and indigenous artists to paint the flora of Texas. He told many of the consolation he had received from the array of natural flowers that blanketed his drilling sites. This colorful aura deeply influenced Davis, and through the San Antonio Art League he volunteered to underwrite a wildflower painting contest to be administered by the league. The award for the first-place painting done by a national artist and prize for the best painting by a Texas artist were, in fact, the largest purchase prizes ever awarded for single works at that time. Davis supported these competitions for three years, contributing a total of $53,000 in purchase awards and donating the winning paintings to the art league. The subject of the ensuing chapter, the Texas Wildflower Competitive Exhibitions, represent Davis's most successful and enduring art venture. They clearly influenced the course of Texas art and established San Antonio as one of the important art centers of the period—not just in the state but in all the country.

The competitions also roughly demarcate the end of Edgar B. Davis's large-scale support of the arts and letters. Although he maintained an avid interest throughout the remainder of his life, of necessity, he gave less financial support to these areas as his own financial affairs became more and more constrained in the years after 1929.

CHAPTER THREE

A Contest Worthy of Flowers

The idea of a national art competition centered upon scenes of Texas wildflowers was that of Edgar Davis, the genesis of which can be traced to his earliest wildcatting experiences in Texas. Even as he first arrived in Texas, during those trying times when he was putting down six successive dry holes in the hills around Luling, Edgar B. Davis was struck by the abundant wildflowers in the drilling fields. The flora of those fields spoke to him, and he connected with these flowers in a special way. He called them "flowers of God."[1] He felt that the verdant and colorful flowers that bloomed all about the Luling area had lifted his spirits in his early wildcatting days and had given him inspiration and courage to continue his pursuits. He resolved that when he was finally successful he would do something to perpetuate their beauty and spirit.

In 1926, at the height of his financial prosperity, Davis remembered his debt to the wildflowers and conceptualized the idea of capturing their array of form and color on canvas. He determined that he would seek the finest American artists to paint these subjects and, in order to encourage their interest and participation, he would offer significant cash prizes for their efforts. He envisioned offering the best of these images for public review and appreciation through a series of open exhibitions.

To handle the details of such a competition, Davis went to Ethel Tunstall Drought, San Antonio's longstanding patron of the arts and president of the San Antonio Art League. Given Davis's refined tastes and interests in the arts, he was almost certainly well acquainted with Drought. She was already a fixture in San Antonio society by the time Davis struck it big in Luling, having assumed the helm of the San Antonio Art League some ten years earlier.

Ethel Drought was in fact a native of old San Antonio, born in the city in 1864.[2] Her artistic credits included the distinction of having been a youthful student of Robert Onderdonk, one of the early pioneers and most influential of Texas artists in the late nine-

Ethel Tunstall Drought. Portrait of Ethel Tunstall Drought, *by Rosamon Niles, 1938. Drought was a formidable president of the San Antonio Art League, a position she held for a quarter of a century. Under her guidance, the league assumed a major leadership role in Texas art in the early part of the century. Courtesy San Antonio Art League*

teenth century.[3] In 1913, she became president of the art league, one of the state's first art organizations, a position she held continuously for the next quarter of a century, until 1938. Drought was a hard-working and visionary leader for the San Antonio Art League, and under her direction, the organization achieved prominence and respect as a leading proponent for the arts in the state. Through her, the league was instrumental in establishing the Witte Museum in 1926, one of

Texas' first modern museums. She was also active and influential in the affairs of the city and was widely known as San Antonio's leading hostess, frequently entertaining local artists and art aficionados in her home, Droughtfels. She was especially known for her Sunday evening gatherings in which the most prominent of San Antonio's art community routinely came together to assay the local art scene and advance the cause of art within the city.[4] Davis was most likely a guest at many such occasions and apparently developed a strong friendship with Drought. Eleanor Onderdonk, the youngest of the famous family of San Antonio artists and later a distinguished art curator for the Witte Museum, references their friendship in a report to the museum board, noting that "not feeling competent to launch the project himself, Mr. Davis (requesting that his name be anonymous) entrusted management to the Art League due to his friendship and admiration of Mrs. Drought."[5] Although it is not known when or in what form Edgar Davis presented his ideas to Drought, it is known that plans for Davis's proposed wildflower competitive art exhibitions were in fact the subject of one of Drought's regular Sunday soirees.[6]

According to Eleanor Onderdonk, Drought viewed the national magnitude of the contest as a "pretty big order" and characterized Davis's contest ideas as "overpowering."[7] However, she also immediately saw the benefits of such a contest for the young San Antonio art community, as well as the significance of such an event for the larger Texas fine arts community, and agreed to take full charge of managing the contests— a task she continued for all three years that Davis sponsored the affair. To his credit, Edgar Davis demonstrated executive genius in selecting the art league and Drought as managers of the contest, for in this association he found competent and enthusiastic partners whose work guaranteed the success of the event.

Also to his credit, Davis repeatedly requested that his name be withheld from association with the contest, but again, according the recollections of Eleanor Onderdonk, "that was impossible to keep secret," at least for the long term.[8]

The first print reference to the Texas Wildflower Competitive Exhibitions came on March 21, 1926, with the *San Antonio Express* headline announcing, "Texas Wildflowers Open Purse of Art Lover for Painting Competition: Anonymous Member San Antonio Art League Offers $6000 for Two Paintings." The article noted that Texas wildflowers "so appealed to a San Antonio man that he has given $6000 to have them painted by the best artists who can be induced to visit Texas and try to reproduce their beauty on canvas."[9] The paper announced the official opening of the contest and declared that it would close "early in 1927," a date later determined by the art league as January 15.[10]

Ethel Drought wasted little time in disseminating information, making announcements to over 340 weekly newspapers in Texas, and contacting numerous national art associations and publications. Rules for the contest were also developed by the art league and issued in a pamphlet that proclaimed that "the Art League of San Antonio Offers $6000 in Cash Prizes for Landscapes in Oil Depicting Texas Wildflowers."[11] Like the press releases before them, the contest rules were widely distributed to art leagues and other associations, as well as directly to practicing artists.

The 1927 contest rules required all artists to use oil as the medium for their work and all paintings to reflect a theme of Texas wildflowers. Canvases were to be of moderate size, ranging from a minimum of 14" by 20" to a maximum of 30" by 40".[12]

The prize of $5,000 was to be provided for the winning painting, and any American artist was eligible for the award if he or she were a member of an "accredited art organization." A $1,000 purchase prize was also to be awarded for the best painting by any artist who was "resident in Texas."[13] Edgar Davis had determined that the winning painting in the national competition would be given to the Lotus Club of New York, a gentleman's social club of which he was a member. The winning painting by a Texas artist was to become the property of the San Antonio Art League.[14]

The response to the announcement was positive and served to stimulate substantial interest in the contest. On September 19, 1926, the *San Antonio Express* reported "some 3000 competing in the Texas Wildflower Landscape contest."[15] While offering encouraging publicity for the fledgling contest, this liberal estimate most likely represented an error in printing. Other estimates reflect about 350 entries in the 1927 contest, representing, nonetheless, a significant number of paintings for the new competition.[16]

The three hundred plus entries were assembled at the Witte Museum, only recently opened, and were reviewed first by a panel of selectors, comprised of a group of local artists and chaired by the English-born, Saint Louis artist Dawson Dawson-Watson. In addition to Dawson-Watson, members of the selection panel included José Arpa, Eleanor Onderdonk, Rolla Taylor, Eloise Polk McGill, Sybil Barron, and Paul Rodda Cook.[17] They selected seventy-seven paintings from the total field of entries for inclusion in the exhibit and competition.[18] From those works selected for exhibition, a group of thirty-five paintings were designated as finalists for the national competition prize of $5,000. Of this, ten artists were from outside the state and twenty-three were Texas artists. The "Texas only" category included forty-two additional canvases representing the spectrum of contemporary artists from throughout the state.[19]

Among the national artists competing for the first prize were Californians Maurice Braun, F. W. Asprien, John Gamble, and Theodore Morgan. Nicholas and Adrian Brewer, a father-son combination from Little Rock, Arkansas, were also included, as were New Orleans artist George Castleden and Jackson, Mississippi, painter Marie Hull. Donald Shuhart of Oklahoma City and Dawson-Watson of Saint Louis rounded out the field of national contenders.[20] Theodore Morgan of San Diego and Dawson Dawson-Watson were quickly drawn up in the festivities that were attendant with the contest, and were apparently pleased enough with the setting that they would make San Antonio their permanent residence following the 1927 competitions. Dawson-Watson continued on the local scene for many years thereafter with noteworthy success as an artist, and Morgan achieved a small degree of local prominence as a newspaper reporter and art critic.

The delegation of Texas artists in this initial competition was wonderfully diverse in its representation of all of the state's major art colonies. Texas artists in the exhibit were led by such established painters as José Arpa (San Antonio), Emma Richardson Cherry (Houston), Edward Eisenlohr (Dallas), Boyer Gonzales (Galveston), and W. Edward Bryan (Dublin). Of the

Texas artists in this first exhibition, San Antonio painters were most heavily represented, with a field of no less than seventeen of the forty-two indigenous artists listed as residents of the city. Presumably, most of these San Antonians were members of the art league, and while most never attained great prominence, the city was well represented by works of some its most accomplished artists. In addition to Arpa, the local contingent included Paul Rodda Cook, Eloise Polk McGill, Rolla Taylor, and Gilbert Neumann, all of whom achieved a modicum of regional acclaim later in their careers. Seven Austin artists were prominently displayed, including Janet Downie, Raymond Everett, and Nannie Huddle. The Houston art colony also had a significant delegation of artists in the exhibit, including Bertha Hellman and Edward Wilkinson, in addition to the aforementioned Emma Richardson Cherry, one of the leading artists in the state at the time. The El Paso art colony was represented by Audley Dean Nicols and Eugene Thurston. Everett Gee Jackson of Mexia, who would later achieve recognition in Southern California for his bright renditions of Mexican subjects, also displayed a painting in the exhibition. Another Texas artist of note in the 1927 exhibition was Mollie L. Crowther, whose painting entitled *A Glorious Morning* was selected for display. Crowther, who was sixty years old at the time of the competitions, had played a prominent role in Texas art history by founding the Christoval artist camp. This summer camp, established in 1921 outside of San Angelo, Texas, had proven to be a major catalyst for art in Texas and had grown to become the largest such gathering of working Texas artists, attracting many of the state's finest painters as instructors and participants. The Texas Wildflower Competitive Exhibition of 1927 would prove to be Crowther's last major exhibit, as she passed away in August of that year.[21]

Alexandre Hogue, who would later become the principal advocate for the Dallas regionalist school, also exhibited his painting entitled *Bear Grass* in the 1927 competition. As for Crowther, 1927 would also be the only time that Hogue would exhibit in the contest. Hogue, a scion of Texas modernists, became seriously disenchanted with the judging. So vexed was he by the judges' obvious conservatism in awarding the prize paintings that he was later moved to express his dissatisfaction in writing. In fact, in a 1929 article in *Southwest Review,* Hogue offered a scathing editorial of the Davis wildflower competitions, deploring the judges and the prize selections.[22]

It was Hogue's thesis that the Eastern judges employed to select the prizewinning paintings were biased and lacking in their appreciation for the contemporary movements that were beginning to influence American art, including his own work. Hogue also contended that Easterners could scarcely understand and appreciate the nuances of a genuine Texas landscape, farm scene, or ranch scene. Thus it was his belief that some of the finest and truest renditions of Texas subjects were overlooked by the judges due to this lack of knowledge and sensitivity to the nature of the Southwest. Although the appreciation of Texas art aficionados for the avant-garde would change in the ensuing years, the selections of the contest judges were probably more compatible with the tastes of the rank-and-file Texan than with the views held by Hogue and his modernist colleagues. While today they may be rightfully criticized for their conservatism and tastes for academic

renderings, the judges assembled by Drought and her colleagues actually comprised a prestigious panel, representing some of the most important art personalities of the time. Led by sixty-six-year-old Charles Curran, the panel carefully reviewed the seventy plus paintings in order to select the two prizewinners. Curran had gained international distinction as the corresponding secretary of the National Academy of Design. He was also a member of the New York Fine Arts Commission and a trustee of the American Fine Arts Society. He was assisted by Henry Snell, member of the New Hope, Pennsylvania, art colony and president of the New York Watercolor Society. Also serving as a member of this elite panel was the internationally renowned Édouard Léon of Paris, recognized as the world's foremost etcher, who was in San Antonio as part of a national tour in which he represented the Beaux Arts in Paris and the French Ministry of Foreign Affairs.[23]

On February 2, 1927, the *San Antonio Light* reported that the paintings would be exhibited at the Witte through March 2 of that year. This article was also the first public reference to Davis as a figure in the contest, acknowledging "the idea of Edgar Davis, donor of the prize, . . . to develop and encourage the work of Texas painters and to invite competition with artists of established reputation." In this same account, the correspondent noted that "every part of Texas is represented in the pictures, as well as practically every well known artist in the state." The reporter further offered the observation "that it is exceedingly interesting to note that many of the pictures receiving the most attention were by artists of little more than local reputation."[24]

Prior to the opening of the exhibition to the general public, the art league hosted a "varnishing day" for all artists whose work had been selected for exhibition. Varnishing day was the artists' final opportunity to view their paintings as they would be displayed and to attend to any last-minute touches, such as varnishing, that would enhance the presentation of their works. In addition to events for the artists, the league hosted preview receptions for civic and business leaders, artists and instructors within the city, and the superintendent and board of education of the San Antonio school district.[25]

The award winners were announced on February 19, 1927, at a luncheon held in the Menger Hotel.[26] Later that evening, Davis offered a dinner party at the Saint Anthony Hotel honoring Drought, officers of the San Antonio Art League, contest judges, and visiting artists. Kelts C. Baker, a vice president of Davis's oil firm, served as the resident host. He arranged for elaborate place settings, including place mats featuring an image of the tower of Mission San José etched by San Antonio artist Bernhardt Wall. Chairman Curran gave a speech on behalf of the contest judges, noting San Antonio's enthusiasm for the arts and pointedly contrasting it with New York's indifference to its own art institutions. In keeping with Davis's tastes and appreciation for the performing arts, the party featured a musical recital and ended with a toast and all singing "For He's a Jolly Good Fellow" in honor of Edgar Davis.[27]

The first prize in the 1927 competition was awarded to Dawson Dawson-Watson for his painting of Texas cactus entitled *The Glory of the Morning*. The $5,000 award brought with it much attention, since it represented the largest cash award for a single painting in an American art competition.

Dawson-Watson was born in London, England, in 1864, the son of an important British artist and illustrator. He first came to the United States in 1893. After a brief return to England and a long period of time spent in the northeastern United States, he moved to Saint Louis in 1904 where he spent eleven years. He made his first trip to San Antonio in 1917 and returned again briefly in 1920. He returned yet again in 1926 upon receiving, while in Boston, Drought's correspondence regarding the contest. To finance his return to San Antonio, he sold a painting for $500. He left Boston within thirty-six hours of his sale and arrived in San Antonio in May of 1926.[28] The artist was an acknowledged lover of the cactus, a lowly plant in Texas, often despised by the ranchers and pioneers of the vicinity. "I worship it . . . kiss my hand to its tiniest bloom. I've painted it inside out, upside down and crosswise," he is reported to have stated. He knew of over four hundred varieties and observed that he had "counted seventy-five species in the grunnels of the Oblate Seminary in the Laurel Heights region of San Antonio."[29]

After his arrival in May through October of 1926, Dawson-Watson executed over seventy different paintings of cacti. *The Glory of the Morning* was actually painted in July, 1926, based on a setting just off Fredericksburg Road near Camp Bullis, Texas. Although he often painted plein air, Dawson-Watson painted this winning canvas in his studio from memory, completing the painting in about three and a half hours. It was, according to him, "the picture I had in mind when I started from Boston to compete for the Texas Wildflower prize. I knew from experience how extraordinarily paintable the cactus is, and I planned to make cactus pictures my contribution to the contest."[30]

Dawson-Watson looked naturally "painterly," tall and mustached, with his most distinguishing outer characteristic his use of a white cloth tied around his neck in lieu of a collar.[31] Boosted by his reception in the community and his success in achieving the first prize, he stayed on, establishing a permanent studio and taking residency in San Antonio. He died in the city in 1939. Even after his death, his work was well regarded. One of his paintings of the Governor's Palace in old San Antonio was permanently displayed in the president's office during the administration of Lyndon B. Johnson.[32]

José Arpa's painting entitled *Verbena* won the first place award for an indigenous artist and received the $1,000 prize. It represented a "flower mead near Helotes, Texas." Described as "perfectly colored," the painting depicts a lush pink field of wildflowers set against a gray sky and the distinguishable terrain of the Texas Hill Country.[33]

Arpa had been a permanent resident of San Antonio since 1923. He was already well established as an international painter prior to moving to the city and had works included among many important collections and museums by the time of the contest. Born in Spain in 1859, Arpa went to Mexico in 1894 and remained a resident there for many years. He first visited San Antonio in his service as a guardian for the children of his good friend, Antonio Quijano. When the Quijano children entered school in San Antonio, Arpa went along as their chaperone and advisor and opened a studio in the city around 1920.[34] He apparently appreciated the area and likened its atmospheric qualities to those of Seville, near where he was born,

and Oaxaca, Mexico. He believed that these cities shared ideal conditions of light and atmosphere for the artist.[35] He was known as a brilliant colorist and became known especially for his ability to skillfully portray the heat and light of the sun, earning him the moniker of "Sunshine Man" in American art circles. A respected and effective art teacher, Arpa ran one of the early art schools in the city and was affectionately referred to by his students as "Papa."[36] In later life, Arpa returned to his native Spain where he died at an advanced age.

In addition to the prizewinning paintings, the judges selected five canvases for designation as honorable mention. These included Audley Dean Nicols's *West Texas Wildflowers*, which Helen Raley described as "vigorous and exquisite in its presentation of desert beauty; expanses of yellow-blossomed broomweed, sage and cactus, tall stalks of varnish-laden ocotillo, all radiant under a typical Texas sky."[37] Also receiving honorable mention were Dallas artist Edward G. Eisenlohr's *Spring Fields at Grand Prairie*, Maurice Braun's *Live Oaks and Bluebonnets*, Theodore J. Morgan's *The Soul of Texas*, and San Antonio artist Mrs. A. J. Bell's *A Cloudy Day*.

The prizewinners and honored paintings, along with eighteen others selected by the judges, completed a suite of twenty-five canvases that were forwarded to New York for display at Avery Hall on the campus of Columbia University. There the collection was provided special accord by Columbia's president, Nicholas Murray Butler, a friend of Edgar B. Davis. In New York, the paintings received many favorable comments and were reported by Drought as "an artistic success."[38] Subsequently, these paintings were displayed in a traveling exhibition in the Texas cities of Abilene, El Paso,

Victoria, Fort Worth, Houston, Denton, and Dallas before returning to San Antonio in late summer. It has been estimated that over eighty thousand people viewed these exhibits, a number that reflects the interest the contest held for Texans during the era.

Thus in his efforts to perpetuate the beauty of the Texas wildflower, and to encourage Texas scenes and artists, Edgar Davis's contest had proven to be a tremendous success. In her report for *Holland's* magazine, Helen Raley summarized the significance of the event: "Seldom has any art contest in the United States roused as much interest. Certainly never in Texas has been or will be again, one of such significance. The generous cash prizes attracted national attention to the beauty of Texas flowers—more abundant and varied than in any state—and scenery. They stimulated the devotion of the two prize winners who 'discovered' southwest Texas years ago; brought other painters to join the art colonies of San Antonio, El Paso, Houston, Dallas, Christoval; and provided the nucleus for future achievement."[39]

With such enthusiasm and widespread support for his first contest, Davis could not but offer to back a bigger and better competition for 1928. On March 27, 1927, the *San Antonio Light* carried Ethel Drought's announcement of an expanded contest, carrying an even larger purse of prizes. In this 1928 competition, in addition to the subject of Texas wildflowers, which was open again to national and indigenous painters, artists were also able to submit canvases in two additional categories: Texas ranch life and Texas cotton fields. Davis offered a total of $14,500 in prize money for this second competition.[40] The 1928 contest provided a total of ten prizes in the four categories. Given the substan-

tial increase and distribution of prize money, the positive publicity afforded the first contest, and the experience gained by the art league in the initial competition, the 1928 event would prove to be a significantly larger contest and the exhibition even more impressive than the first. However, as the stakes increased for both money and recognition, the 1928 competitions were also destined to become the instrument of considerable controversy within the San Antonio art community.

In announcing the expanded 1928 contest, Drought directed correspondence to 437 Texas newspapers. The presidents of 825 art organizations received the contest rules and entry blanks. Letters were sent to 445 individual artists. In addition, the art league used the medium of radio for the first time with announcements on stations WOAI and WCAR.[41] Both the *San Antonio Light* and *Express* carried articles announcing the event.

The second-year rules for the contest remained the same as the first except that paintings could be entered by any artist in any of the first three categories of wildflowers, ranch life, and cotton fields. The fourth category, based also on the theme of Texas wildflowers, was again reserved exclusively for Texas artists.

The category of wildflowers open to any artist listed four prizes, ranging from $1,000 for fourth place to $2,500 for first prize. There were two prizes of $1,500 and $1,000 for each of the other three categories. In addition, ten honorable mention prizes of $100 were to be awarded.[42]

The second-year response was even more positive than the first. In January the San Antonio press included a headline heralding, "World Famous Send Entries into Contest." Referring to the event as "a new chapter in the history of Texas artistry," the news re-

Sunny Afternoon, *Lawson Blackmon, 1928. Courtesy San Antonio Art League*

ported receipt of paintings from "notables such as Oscar Berninghaus (St. Louis and Taos), W. Herbert Dunton (Taos), Isabel B. Cartwright (Philadelphia), Joseph Birren (Chicago), Henry Keller (Cleveland) and Benjamin Brown of California."[43]

In all, the 1928 contest received about 460 canvases from 211 artists, and of these a jury identified some 91 paintings representing 59 artists for exhibition and competition.[44] The jury of selection was again chaired by Dawson Dawson-Watson and included Eleanor Onderdonk, who had been hired by the Witte during the previous year to curate the museum's growing collection, Mary Bonner, Emma Richardson Cherry, James Chillman, Edward Eisenlohr, and Samuel Gideon.[45]

The paintings for exhibition represented artists from fifteen states other than Texas, attracting for the first time artists from the Eastern Seaboard, including established colonies in New York (Arthur Woeffle), Philadelphia (Isabel Branson Cartwright), and Connecticut (H. C. Schlichting). Artists from the California school were well represented (Benjamin Brown, William Silva, Power O'Malley), as were members of the Taos art colony (Oscar Berninghaus, W. Herbert Dunton). Additionally, works of artists from Arizona, Arkansas, Indiana, Nebraska, Mississippi, Ohio, Minnesota, Delaware, and Oklahoma were accepted for exhibit.

Among Texas artists, San Antonio was still the city of greatest influence with no less than twenty-six local canvases included in the exhibit. This included Dawson-Watson and Theodore Morgan, first-year winners who had relocated to the city the preceding year. Most of Texas' accomplished artists, including Eisenlohr, Richardson Cherry, Arpa, Gonzales, and Bryan were again represented. Ella Mewhinney of Holland, Texas, returned for the exhibition. New to the Texas group were Marie Haines of College Station, Rolla Taylor of San Antonio, Coreen Mary Spellman of Denton, and Robert Wood of San Antonio. Also new was Kindred McLeary, a twenty-six-year-old professor of architecture at the University of Texas, whose entry would create the great "stir" of the contest.[46] The competition again attracted a significant delegation from the El Paso colony, including Lewis Teel, Muriel Ruth Gudger, Berla Iyone Emeree, Seth Floyd

Crews, and Mary Roberta Nichols, in addition to previous honorable mention winner Audley Dean Nicols.

As the paintings were assembled for exhibit, controversy reared its head within the San Antonio art community. First, charges were aired by John C. Filippone, president of the San Antonio Art Guild, who asserted that artist members of his organization had been the victims of "discrimination" by the art league's panel of selectors. Filippone was one of the founders of the guild, which was composed of San Antonio artists who had disassociated themselves from the San Antonio Art League when it became too social for their interests. As evidence in support of his charges, Filippone reported that only one of the guild's members, Gilbert Neumann, had been selected for exhibition.[47]

This debate was overshadowed, however, by the uproar created upon the viewing of young Kindred McLeary's painting entitled *Cotton.* The painting portrayed the obvious fantasy of a pair of African-American field hands, possibly celebrating the conclusion of a harvest day. It presented a nude African-American woman provocatively positioned at the end of a field row, juxtaposed against the field hand's full sack of cotton, and overseen by his banjo-playing colleague. The painting at once created a sensation among members of the conservative fine arts community, and the merits of the piece were debated in the press. Led by Eloise Polk McGill, one of the San Antonio artists displayed in the exhibition and an art league officer, invitations went out to an interdenominational panel of local ministers to view the painting in order to pass on its moral qualities. McGill charged that the painting was "sexually vulgar."[48]

Spring Day, *Paul Rodda Cook, 1928. Courtesy San Antonio Art League*

Meanwhile, a group of local and out-of-town artists banded together in defense of the painting, claiming that charges of "obscenity" and "indecency" were a simple case of hysteria. José Arpa declared the painting to be "beautiful," with excellent color and line.

Mary Bonner, San Antonio's internationally acclaimed etcher and a member of the selection panel, defended the painting as well as the artist. The painting she described as "simply a bit of music; jazz, perhaps, but music." She characterized the piece as a "modernistic, decorative work." Even Aline Rather, the supervisor of art for the San Antonio public schools, came to the painting's defense. "I don't think McLeary intended to be vulgar or immoral. I think he simply wanted to startle the conservatives by putting something different into their midst. The colors are well-handled and it has good balance."[49]

The critics, however, were relentless in their opposition. Mrs. A. J. Bell, the recipient of an honorable mention award in the previous year's competition, declined to judge the picture as immoral but stated that "it is certainly gross." Her associate, Miriam Edstrom, stated that the painting was "ugliness, well drawn." Minnie Hollis Haltom was more adamant in her critique. "It is the picturization of naughty dreams, and if 'Cotton' is an example of the standard of art for San Antonio, I can't afford to exhibit. It is most obscene and it repels." She went further to pronounce the painting as "ultra-modern, entirely too much so," and expressed her observations regarding the declining popularity of ultramodernism in the Eastern art scene. The principal of San Antonio's Thomas Nelson Page Junior School explained *Cotton* as "Freudian exposure," declaring that it "makes an immoral appeal." Even museum director Ellen Schulz offered her observation that the picture looked "like wall paper that you don't like," and "consequently, I have been keeping away from it."[50]

Typical of the press, the *San Antonio Express* sensed an opportunity to capitalize on the fervor created by the piece and ran a front-page photograph of the painting, entitling the image "Here Is the Painting about Which Controversy Arises in Contest," and described a "violent controversy raging around the painting." While controversy was indeed raging about his work in San Antonio, McLeary was back at home in Austin confined to his bed with an attack of bronchitis. There, he declared his amusement with the entire situation: "The critics who would remove my picture are taking themselves and the painting entirely too seriously." He felt that "there is nothing deep about the picture. It is easily understood if one looks at it in the right light. I painted it to express a mood, and I assure you it has no hidden meaning." McLeary, however, left the painting's fate to the discretion of the judges, indicating that he would "make no effort to prevent its removal, if the judges believe that it is out of place."[51]

Apparently the judges ruled in McLeary's favor and allowed *Cotton* a place in the exhibit, for a later news account leads with "Cotton to Be Kept in Exhibit."[52] In the following years McLeary left Texas to join the faculty at Carnegie Institute of Technology in Pittsburgh, where he remained for the duration of his career. He received considerable recognition in the northeast as a muralist and died an untimely death in 1949 as a result of a fall from the roof of his studio in Pittsburgh.[53] The fate of the painting *Cotton* is unknown.

The fact that such a painting could be included by the judges of selection, coupled with the art guild's claim of discrimination, fueled the fires of contention regarding the ethics and advisability of allowing competing artists to double as selection jurists. Although this was a common practice in Eastern art competitions, several artists expressed concern that the practice was inappropriate for the Davis competition since there was "so much money at stake."[54] At least one

Wild Poppies on the Creek Bank, *William Silva, 1928. Courtesy San Antonio Art League*

editorial in city newspapers, entitled "Art Turns Spotlight on Us," proposed that one of two courses of action be pursued in order to assure "greater harmony" and to assure that the "cause of art is profited." Specifically, the writer suggested that the league should either hang all canvases entered in the contest or disqualify selection officials from also competing in the contest.[55] This matter was successfully resolved in the subsequent competition by essentially accepting both recommendations.

It was in this maelstrom of controversy that the judges began their work to select the prizewinning paintings. The judges of awards for 1928 again represented a collection of elite names in American art. Alphaeus P. Cole of New York chaired the judging panel. He was assisted by the noted artist Abbot Graves of Maine, a member of the prestigious National Academy of Design, and by Ellsworth Woodward, president of the Southern States Art League and director of Newcomb College in New Orleans. Unfazed by controversy, they completed their tasks, giving the entire field of paintings high compliments for the overall quality of the works.[56]

Once again the 1928 exhibit opened to an enthusiastic public reception, and attendance was good. At the awards luncheon held at the venerable old Menger Hotel, Alphaeus Cole spoke of Davis's patronage of the event, positing that "he is probably contributing more toward the welfare of art both locally and nationally than any other American millionaire, since he is encouraging living artists." He also conveyed something of the national significance of the event when he declared "that the San Antonio contest has turned even the eyes of the New York art colony toward wildflower painting in Texas."[57]

The winning painting in the open category based on the theme of Texas wildflowers was by thirty-seven-year-old Adrian Brewer of Little Rock, Arkansas. His landscape entitled *In a Bluebonnet Year* offered great color and light in its presentation of Texas' favored wildflower. Brewer, originally from Minnesota, had come to Texas with his father, also an artist, to compete for the contest prize. In attempting to capture the bluebonnets, Adrian and his father executed numerous field studies during the previous spring. His father, frustrated with his own efforts, gave up the task as "hopeless." The young Adrian persisted in his work, achieving mastery of the genre. His first-place finish in this category gave him instant notoriety in Texas as well as the nation. He continued to paint floral landscapes for several more years, selling over twenty-five bluebonnet pieces through a prestigious New York gallery.[58]

William Silva of Carmel, California, received the $1,500 second-place prize in this category for his *Wild Poppies on the Creek Bank*. José Arpa, whose painting had succumbed to Dawson-Watson's cactus piece the preceding year, offered his own colorful rendition of the Texas cactus in the third-place painting entitled *Cactus Flowers*. Californian Benjamin Brown received the fourth prize with his bluebonnet theme entitled *When Bluebonnets Bloom*.

In the category of ranch life, Cleveland's Henry Keller received top honors with his *Ranch Life, Western Texas*. It was the judges' first choice among all prizewinning paintings. The painting, an "unusually strong and vigorous picture, rich in coloring," featured men on horses fording a stream in the shadow of tall, straight trees.[59] Power O'Malley, of Los Angeles, received second place in this category with his painting entitled *Evening on X Ranch, Texas*.

Isabel Branson Cartwright of Philadelphia won the initial award for Texas cotton fields. Her *Cotton Picking Time* was a bright and colorful rendition of the theme. San Antonio artist Lawson Blackmon won second place with *Sunny Afternoon*.

In the wildflower category reserved for Texas artists only, Theodore Morgan, a recent transplant from San Diego to Texas, won first place with the painting

Mexican Heather and Salt Cedar. Morgan, who had by now begun to pen a regular art column in the local newspaper entitled "In San Antonio's World of Art," was apparently grateful for his own winnings and simultaneously concerned about the small tempest of controversies accompanying the exhibition. He admonished the San Antonio art community and wrote of Davis's patronage in his column: "Mr. Davis' kindness, generosity and foresight is seen by his performances that no man can ever think otherwise, and it would be ungrateful for the slightest thing to ever be brought to him which might disturb him. Realize how few such persons that [there] are in the world, and that of all the cities in the United States, he selected San Antonio. Understand that there was not the slightest selfish nature behind this gift. His wonderful love of mankind, a part of his Creator's being, is perhaps the reason for it. I sense a deeply religious motive, as gifts like this can only emanate from a true understanding of the celestial laws."[60] In addition to Morgan's canvas, Audley Dean Nicols received a second-place award for his painting entitled *Texas Plains.*

The honorable mentions also included many noteworthy artists. Oscar Berninghaus was recognized for his *Winter in the Panhandle.* Joseph Birren of Chicago was acknowledged for his painting entitled *Floral Glory of Palo Duro Canyon.* W. Herbert Dunton's stunning painting, *The Horse Wrangler,* was awarded honorable mention, as were Indiana's Louis O. Griffith's *Spring's Enchantment* and *Rounding Them Up* by H. C. Schlichting. Texan Edward Eisenlohr (*When the Year Is Young*), Ella Mewhinney (*Shadows*), Margaret Tupper (*The Texas Range*), and Rolla Taylor (*Blue Fields*) were also recognized.

Despite its points of controversy, the second con-test was heralded as a great success. Newspaper coverage was widespread, and the Texas press acknowledged Davis for his gesture, which brought increased recognition of both the beauty of the state and the talents of Texas artists. This theme was underscored by the national press, including the *Christian Science Monitor* and the *New York Evening Post.* Of course, not all of the press was good. The *Chicago News* categorized the contest as "third-rate art competing for first-class prize money." The *New York Times,* upon receiving the exhibition in that city, characterized the paintings as "unimpressive." The *New Yorker* dubbed the canvases "assembly line productions," proclaiming that "these paintings took $15,000 of some man's money."[61] Perhaps, however, *Time* magazine best exemplified the prejudice and stereotypes against southwestern subjects that existed in eastern circles when it editorialized that "art has no boundaries. It may flower at anytime in any place. In the US, the state of Texas has never been closely associated with the production of good, or even mediocre paintings. In that state, nevertheless, monetary prizes, which in amount probably exceed those ever offered elsewhere, are offered for paintings of Texas wildflowers, ranch life, and field scenes. They are offered by Edgar B. Davis, famed millionaire and sole support of *The Ladder,* Manhattan drama to which admission is free."[62]

Despite these adverse commentaries by some of the national press, the preponderance of the publicity was favorable and reinforced Davis and his regional art competitions. As a culminating event for the season, Davis hosted another lavish party at the Saint Anthony Hotel for all associated with the competitive exhibitions. Described by the artist Clara Caffrey Pancoast as a "riot of colors," the event was Davis's venue for announcing yet a third competition—larger again in scope and extending his own record cash prizes by offering a total of $31,500 for awards.[63] In continuing the contest, Davis, who was now referred to by the San Antonio press as the "Fairy Godfather of Artists," announced that he was "convinced that the master canvas has not yet been painted and that it would come forth as the brainchild of some artist through stimulating influence."[64]

After exhibiting again at Columbia in New York, the 1928 winners, twenty-eight paintings in all, toured the cities of Fort Worth, Dallas, Denton, and Abilene.[65] They were to be returned to the Witte Museum in time for a fall exhibition in conjunction with the meeting of the National Federation of Women's Clubs.[66] While in Abilene, the exhibit drew the unanimous praise of the art faculty of that community's three universities—Claire Tate of McMurry College, Mrs. C. B. Locke of Abilene Christian University, and Mrs. A. M. Carpenter of Simmons College.[67]

The 1929 contest was highly acclaimed and the most successful of all three in terms of the number, variety, and quality of paintings. The *American Magazine of Art* reported that so many artists arrived in San Antonio from all parts of the country that "the smock and paint box were as familiar upon the streets as the five gallon hats of the cowboys."[68]

This time, the jury of selection was chaired by Robert Vonnoh, the notable New York artist, and included Gutzom Borglum and Mary Bonner, as well as Emma Richardson Cherry, Evelyn Byers Bessell, James Chillman, and Frederick Brown, all of Houston.[69] The jury reviewed almost 690 canvases, selecting a record 139 paintings for exhibition.[70]

Besides an expanded representation of Texas artists, the exhibition field featured thirty-seven artists from fifteen states and the District of Columbia, as well as two artists residing in Mexico. Texans new to the competition included Xavier Gonzalez, the nephew of José Arpa; Peter Hohnstedt and Harry Anthony DeYoung, both of San Antonio; as well as Frank Klepper and Jessiejo Eckford of Dallas. Max Bachofen of Castroville, Marie Cronin of Bartlett, and San Antonio painter Charlotte Reeves were also new to the competition.

Nine artists from California, including Maurice Braun and William Silva of Carmel, Frank Tenney Johnson of Alhambra, and a young Millard Sheets of Hollywood, were represented in the competition. The Taos and Santa Fe colonies were again well represented in the exhibition, including works by Catherine Critcher, W. Herbert Dunton, Oscar Berninghaus, E. Martin Hennings, and Joseph Fleck of Taos. Works by Santa Fe's Jozef Bakos were also included. Four New York artists were displayed, including Eliot Clark, Glenn Newell, Anne Goldthwaite, and Power O'Malley. Paintings from five artists from Louisiana were exhibited in the competitions, including a prizewinning piece by Louis Raynaud.

Due to the unusually large number of entries, the opening of the exhibit was delayed a day, but it did not deter attendance, as the *San Antonio Express* reported 5,000 viewers on February 4, portraying the sizable crowds as evincing "unusual interest" in the selected paintings.[71] Later, on February 28, the same paper reported Eleanor Onderdonk's estimate of 10,000 viewers during the previous three days.[72]

The judges for the 1929 contest were named, in-

Texas Fields, *Maurice Braun, 1929. Courtesy San Antonio Art League*

cluding two veteran contest officials—Alphaeus P. Cole and Abbott Graves—who had presided over the 1928 contest. Joining them on the panel was Hermann Dudley Murphy of Lexington, Massachusetts, a faculty member at Harvard's School of Architecture and a "nationally known painter of landscapes and watercolors."[73]

In the open category for wildflower paintings, E. Martin Hennings of Chicago (and of the Taos art colony) won first prize for his painting *Thistle Blossoms*, a brilliant rendition of a mass of wild poppies in the midst of a landscape. The second prize was awarded to Marie Hull of Jackson, Mississippi, for her portrayal of Spanish daggers entitled *Texas Field Flowers.* Californian Maurice Braun took third-place honors with a painting entitled *Texas Fields.* Isabel Branson Cartwright of Philadelphia (and sometimes Terrell, Texas) won fourth place with her painting *Wild Poppies.* Peter Hohnstedt of San Antonio was awarded the fifth prize of $1,500 for *Evening Shades.* L. O. Griffith of Nashville, Indiana, (and sometimes Dallas) received the sixth-place award based on his work entitled *Tranquil Afternoon.* Finally, seventh place was awarded to National Academician Eliot Clark of New York City for his *Red-Bud and Wild Plum* landscape.

In the ranch life category, first prize went to New Yorker C. Glenn Newell for *Upper Range.* This painting was described by Marie Seacord Lilly in her article on the competitions as a "lovely picture depicting a bunch of cattle on the crest of a small upland hill in the gray light of early dawn."[74] Alexandre Hogue, however, referred to Newell's award as the "outstanding blunder of the present display," chastising the piece as a "misty pastoral of New England dairy stock posed in the usual Newell way in New England hills."[75]

Millard Sheets was a little over twenty-one years old at the time he entered the Davis competition. He was discouraged and without sufficient funds to study more. His painting *The Old Goat Ranch* gained him the $1,750 second prize, the proceeds of which he used to travel to Europe and continue his art studies.[76] The painting was a popular one in the exhibition and was described by the *Express's* correspondent as "striking" and "a painting fairly vibrant with life and color and the suggestion of movement." It was also a painting, according to the press accounts, that could be considered "thoroughly modern in technique."[77]

Oscar Berninghaus's *Peaceful Life on the Ranch* was awarded third place in this category. *Texas Night Riders* by California artist Frank Tenney Johnson, portraying two horsemen riding into evening camp, was given fourth-place honors. The painting was typical of Johnson's twilight scenes with its soft coloring. The *Express* account declared the painting as one of the "beautiful paintings shown with ranch life as the subject" and noted that the piece evidenced "much poetry in its conception and treatment."[78] Johnson's painting was based upon his visits to the SMS (Svante Magnus Swenson) Ranch near Stamford, Texas.[79]

Finally, W. Herbert Dunton of Taos offered his *Old Texas* as a fifth-place winner. Dunton, who had worked as a cowboy in his youth, painted a lone cowboy driving a herd of rangy longhorn cattle across a shallow river bed. In the background is a vast West Texas landscape. The painting captured in color and theme the isolation and beauty of the cowboy's work.

The cotton paintings were also of high quality. José Arpa received first place for *Picking Cotton,* a picture of Mexican cotton laborers described as "remarkable in its fidelity of detail and coloring."[80] Oscar Berninghaus also netted a second-place prize in the cotton competition for his painting entitled *Cotton Picking.* Third place went to Louis Raynaud of New Orleans, Louisiana, for his depiction of African-American children entitled *Picaninnies in Cotton.* Nicholas Brewer, Adrian's father, who had earlier forsaken bluebonnet painting, apparently gained a knack for cotton subjects, as he won fourth place for *The Cotton Harvest.* The ever-present Dawson Dawson-Watson drew fifth-place honors for his harvest scene entitled *Early Morning.*

In the Texas-only wildflower competition, Dawson-

Texas Wild Flowers, *Marie Hull, 1929. Courtesy San Antonio Art League*

Watson again garnered first-place honors with his cactus entitled *The Bouquet.* Peter Hohnstedt received second place for *Sunshine and Shadow,* and the Ella Mewhinney painting *Texas Wild Flowers* was awarded third place in this division. Jessiejo Eckford's rendition of the Texas cactus, *Prickly Pear,* was given fourth prize.

Honorable mentions were given to Paul Rodda Cook (*The Lindner Ranch*), Harry Anthony DeYoung (*Twilight Silhouettes*), Henry Keller (*Irrigating Cotton Fields along the Rio Grande*), Frank Klepper (*Texas Plumes*),

Peaceful Life on the Ranch, *Oscar E. Berninghaus, 1929. Courtesy San Antonio Art League*

Theodore J. Morgan (*Spring [Laurel and Mesquite]*), Audley Dean Nicols (*Spring in the Panhandle*), Power O'Malley (*The Lone Star*), William Silva (*Rain Lilies*), Jo Stephen Ward (*When Winter Comes*), and Mrs. Fred Weisser (*Bluebonnets*). In addition, Xavier Gonzalez made his professional debut in oils with the painting *Twilight.* It was credited by the press as having the "strong colors and brightness characteristic of his better known watercolors."[81] This painting was purchased by the art league.

No doubt the quality and range of works presented in the third competition more closely approximated Edgar Davis's original vision of the competition. The third year of the contest had indeed stimulated interest in Texas subjects and had lured many more artists of national acclaim to the state. The competitions were instrumental in casting San Antonio as the premiere art center in the South.

It was at this height of success, however, that Davis made his decision to discontinue the wildflower competitions. Whether driven by financial setbacks or due to his interests in a comparable national competition, Edgar Davis determined that the 1929 competition would be the last. He delivered his decision via telegram, which was read by Ethel Drought at the awards ceremony. In it he noted, "I am not prepared to continue the contest at this time, and yet from a beginning of appreciation of Texas wildflowers has come a desire to see a country-wide movement to depict American life with a view of establishing eventually a truly representative national museum of art in Washington. I hope to be able to bring this to your attention in an effective manner at some future time."[82]

On March 6, Davis hosted what was then described as the "most beautiful and elaborate dinner ever given in San Antonio," as for the last time he entertained the artists, judges, art league officials, and local dignitaries at the Saint Anthony Hotel. The approximately one hundred twenty guests enjoyed the crystal, candles, and flowers that elegantly brandished the Tapestry Room in the grand old hotel. After dinner, the crowd was entertained by quartet members performing "In a Parisian Garden" and a violinist who played "Slavonic Fantasy" by Dvorak. The highlight of the evening's entertainment was Mme. Marie Ascarra's balcony scene from *Romeo and Juliet* and, after a costume change, her rendition of the trial scene from *The Merchant of Venice.*[83]

Once again, all of the award-winning paintings from this exhibition, along with the eleven winners of the 1928 contest, were placed on tour of the state including Texas A&M College, Dallas, Fort Worth, Abilene, Houston, Austin, and Victoria. From there they would go for the last time to Columbia University in New York and subsequently return to the league's home at the Witte in San Antonio.

With that, the wildflower art competitions were over. Together they had represented a remarkable series of art events that had gained national acclaim for the state and for the city of San Antonio, set on the edge of the Texas Hill Country. The competitions also represented Davis's last major foray into the arts. Beset with financial difficulties dwindling his fortune, Davis now focused his every attention on regaining the strength of his financial position. He maintained an avid interest in the fine arts and intended to offer patronage again, once financially able to do so. In 1935, in a letter to Eleanor Onderdonk, he conveyed, "I am glad to know that the pictures have meant a great deal to the people who come to the museum, and when I

The Cotton Harvest, *Nicholas Brewer, 1929. Courtesy San Antonio Art League*

Prickly Pear, *Jessiejo Eckford, 1929. Courtesy San Antonio Art League*

succeed at Buckeye—if the Success comes in time—I have promised myself to give $100,000 at the Centennial for the prize competition. Just now I am as broke as broke can be, but the Good God always has pulled me through these emergencies, and at Buckeye, I Be-lieve I have far and away the biggest thing of my industrial life."[84]

Buckeye, of course, was never really profitable for Davis, and he died with the development of this property still paramount in his mind.

CHAPTER FOUR

Postscripts and Reflections

Even after he discontinued the wildflower competitions, Edgar B. Davis remained a high-profile figure in the Texas oil industry as well as in the nation's rubber industry. His generosity and character made him a popular and appealing persona in the state, and he was revered as a genuine hero in Caldwell and Guadalupe counties. His financial fortunes eventually fell upon bad times, and in the years after 1930, he lived "for almost twenty years in a tangled world of bankruptcy actions, referees, special masters, foreclosures, garnishee trouble, writs, contentious lawyers, and so on."[1]

As a postscript to his business life, Davis continued to wildcat for oil for the remainder of his career. With unbridled enthusiasm he continued to explore new fields and drill oil, albeit with only modest success. Bolstered by his faith, he lived believing that each new wildcat well that he drilled would blow in with resources that would dwarf his earlier exploits, especially the leases he had secured at Buckeye on the Texas coast. In later years he became increasingly obsessed with finding deep oil, believing that the deeper the well the more bountiful the reserves. He pursued deep oil interests in the Luling area, but particularly in the Buckeye field. Buckeye was, in fact, Davis's last major development effort, and he drilled to almost eight thousand feet in the course of completing his only major well there, the Stoddard No. 1. The Stoddard well was a phenomenal one, producing one hundred thousand barrels of oil by the end of its first year. After the Stoddard discovery well, Davis became so excited about the prospects of his leases in the vicinity that he offered the entirety of his Buckeye properties for sale in 1932 for the asking price of twenty million dollars.[2]

His mission and strong religious beliefs still motivated him. So encouraged was he with the potential at Buckeye that he was prompted to write his assistant, David Figart, to comment on his belief that the field would bring immense wealth and, as a consequence, elevate him into his dream of the presidency. Apparently, Davis's renewed enthusiasm was based upon his estimate of the significance of his strike at Buckeye, as well as his view of the scope and magnitude of gifts he could dispense as the Buckeye moneys rolled in. From this, Davis surmised a groundswell of popular support that he believed would usher him to the nation's highest office. To Davis's regret, however, the largest bid for his coastal properties was a paltry one million dollar offer from Humble Oil Company in 1935. He declined the offer, gambling unsuccessfully on his Buckeye holdings until the end of his life. Besides the Stoddard well, Davis found only one additional producer in the Buckeye field, despite a dozen tries. The field never materialized and Davis's profits were far outstripped by expenses.[3]

With continued drilling expenses and only modest production, Davis's financial and political fortunes eventually waned during the latter half of the thirties. In 1935 the United North and South Development Company was in bankruptcy court. Davis barely held on through legal maneuverings and loans from former associates and partners, including the Luling Foundation.[4] To make matters worse, he was involved in an ongoing court battle with the state of Massachusetts for back taxes that he allegedly owed that state. Edgar Davis had strenuously contested these taxes since he had asserted his official residency to be in Texas as early as 1926, and in conformance with Massachusetts law, he felt that he owed no debt to that state. Although he could have settled this tax dispute for a relatively small sum, the issue became a matter of principle for Davis. He related to his associates: "When I said I was a citizen of Texas in 1926, I either lied or I didn't. If I lied, then I owe them the entire amount. But I didn't lie, and I don't owe them a cent."[5]

Nonetheless, after years of litigation, suit, and counter suit in Massachusetts and in Texas, Davis finally lost his case with Massachusetts in 1937 before the Supreme Court of Texas, where he was defended by no less than former governor Dan Moody. Persistent to the end, Davis appealed to the United States Supreme Court, which refused to hear the case. Having thus secured its victory in court, the state of Massachusetts delayed in filing for payment, instead waiting to claim its back taxes from the Davis estate. In this sense, Davis secured a small moral victory by avoiding payments of what he considered to be unjust taxes.[6]

Davis struggled to hold on to the remnants of his crumbling drilling empire until his death. He continued to pursue oil, continued to believe that another fortune would present itself to him for the purposes of others. He also continued to seek his illusive dream of an international rubber cartel through which he could secure for America a reliable supply and stable price for this critical industrial product. Although involved in rubber ventures throughout the thirties and even well into the forties with such giants as Frank Sierberling and Cyrus Eaton, Davis's dream of a consolidated rubber cartel never materialized, and his financial position and influence in the rubber business mirrored his declining fortunes in the oil field.[7]

Given his financial misfortunes, one of Davis's most exciting ideas in the arts was never actualized. The national art competition and museum depicting scenes of American life, which he had introduced so dramatically at the conclusion of his wildflower competitions, fell by the wayside. We are left to conjecture as to exactly what the oilman had in mind. However, given the success of his San Antonio exhibitions, he no doubt foresaw a similar competition on a grand scale that would have offered an unparalleled boost to American art during the period. Given his continued interest in national office, Davis may have also recognized that his sponsorship of such a spectacular American art event could potentially present him with a popular national forum, and thus offer a new route to the presidency. Regrettably, the economics of the Depression kept him from capitalizing on the project and achieving his ends—whether they were social or political.

In 1930, in the aftermath of the wildflower competitions, Edgar Davis was honored by the city of San Antonio and the San Antonio museum board when the Edgar B. Davis Gallery was dedicated at the Witte as a permanent home for his collection of prize paintings. These he had placed in San Antonio on permanent loan to the art league, and upon his death, permanent title was passed to this organization. Ethel Drought presided over the dedication ceremonies, and Davis reluctantly bowed to the naming of the facility after him.[8] He was apparently uncomfortable over this formal acknowledgment. In 1935, he addressed some of this concern when he wrote to Eleanor Onderdonk regarding an upcoming exhibit of the paintings in San Antonio: "I am going to ask you to excuse me from writing anything for the catalog and please do not call it the 'Davis Gallery' or give me any publicity whatever. Anything that comes to me is of the Spirit—I have come to see with Emerson, that of myself, I am nothing, but the Light is all. Consequently, I feel that any attempt to accept credit for myself would be a violation of the Spirit which has made possible whatever has been accomplished."[9]

Even after he was forced to curtail his financial support of the San Antonio Art League, Edgar Davis remained in close touch with the activities of the organization. Without Davis's financial backing, however, the San Antonio art community, which had burst so dramatically upon the national scene in the days of the competitions, lost a degree of momentum. Despite retaining a leadership role in statewide art affairs, San Antonio lost ground to Dallas in the thirties as the undisputed center of Texas art.

Edgar Davis continued a warm and lasting correspondence with Eleanor Onderdonk. Since joining the Witte as its curator of collections in 1927, Onderdonk had played an instrumental role in the competitions and had offered competent, enthusiastic care of the prizewinning paintings that Davis had placed on permanent loan to the art league. It is apparent from their letters that each maintained a mutual regard for the other, and it is also clear that Onderdonk was fastidious in her reports to Davis on the status of "his" paintings. Friends to the end, Onderdonk was in attendance at Davis's funeral, and wrote later to a Virginia friend that "it is very sad to think that Edgar Davis is no more."[10]

Davis also maintained a continuing admiration for Ethel Drought, who died in 1944 at the age of seventy-nine. He must have certainly respected this special woman for the excellent job that she had done for him during her days with the competitions. She left a remarkable record of accomplishment for the art league and for the city, and was eulogized as one of the builders of San Antonio.[11]

In 1965, officers of the league, in an effort to make more space at the Witte for its burgeoning collection of Texas art, engaged a Houston art consultant to select a group of its paintings for sale. Employing a criterion described in art league documents as "unfathomable to this day," fifteen of the paintings from the Davis collection were included in this lot and were sold.[12] The whereabouts of most of the paintings are unknown at this time. In 1970, the San Antonio Art League withdrew from its long association with the Witte Museum but continues today as an important force for the visual arts within the city.[13]

In his later years, after the depletion of his personal fortune, Edgar Davis, by then an aging bachelor, lived in genteel poverty in a small farm cottage on the Luling farm. He had lost his elegant home, The House in the Oaks, in Luling, putting it up as collateral on a note he could not repay. When news of his loss came to the townspeople of Luling, several instigated a mass meeting to buy back the house and its contents and return it to Davis. But Davis would have none of this, attending the meeting himself and declaring, "If you do this thing, I will leave Luling and never come back," a threat his friends and neighbors in Luling took to heart.[14] Subsequently, Davis turned over the property in good order to the San Antonio realtor who was to dispose of his home. The House in the Oaks was soon reduced to virtual rubble, however, due to a series of mysterious acts of vandalism.[15] The culprits were never apprehended by local law enforcement officials, but it seemed fitting to most citizens of Luling that, if their beloved Edgar Davis could not reside in the grand old home, then, really, no one else should ever be able to do so. Earlier, Davis had also lost his Buzzards Bay estate, The House on the Sand, when it was destroyed by hurricane in 1938, taking with it many valuable art works and collectibles from his international excursions.[16]

There can be no doubt that Edgar Davis was revered in his adopted hometown, and he was a frequent and charming visitor about the community of Luling. Riley Froh, the Davis biographer who came of age in this small town and had the privilege of knowing Davis personally, provides a most insightful description of the aging gentleman's presence in Luling in those latter years of his life:

> Having been a legend in his own time for so long, as a fading septuagenarian during the last half of the 1940's, he gravitated into a misplaced New England lost leaf, a quaint personage known by every citizen, young and old, in a little town of 4,000 which boasted him as its first citizen.
>
> He would have been distinct anywhere, but he was particularly atypical in Luling. For instance, he had a well-practiced courtesy and style marked by years of cultivated living in business and social circles in Texas, New York, Massachusetts, Ohio, England, and the Far East. For years people had deferred to him, to his judgment, his opinion, and this habit was observed by others as is often the case with celebrities. He never lost his ability to recount a fascinating story based on some incident during years of travel throughout a long and exciting life, and his many world experiences gave him a rich storehouse of anecdotes set in locales from Wall Street to interior Sumatra. Never losing his sparkling sense of humor, he would insist good-naturedly that his baldness was not from worrying over money, or he would proclaim that he intended to marry and have children at the proper time. Davis was a fine conversationalist in the old sense of the word; that is, he was a good listener. Regularly, the United North and South headquarters boasted the brightest intellectual gathering in town.[17]

As the United States fell into the Second World War, the seventy-year-old Davis again felt compelled to intervene in world affairs. He dusted off his strategic bombing plan that he and his associate David Figart had developed in the final days of World War I and proceeded to market it again as a method for crippling the German war machine and restoring peace on the international front. As he had done while an executive of U.S. Rubber in 1916, Davis persistently sought and received audiences with military and government leaders, using his many influential friends and acquaintances. Texas Senator W. Lee O'Daniel arranged for Davis to visit with England's ambassador, Lord Halifax, and Senator Tom Connally obtained for him an audience with the Sub-Committee on War and Peace Aims of the United States and Allies. Davis sought, however, an audience with President Roosevelt himself for purposes of discussing the strategic plan.[18] While his presidential audience never came, the Allies did indeed begin to pursue a strategy similar to that advanced by Davis and Figart. That approach achieved results strikingly similar to those the old oilman had predicted and is today credited as one of the principal strategies that accelerated the decline of Germany and promoted the end of the war on the European front.

In 1947, on the silver anniversary of his discovery of the Luling field, Edgar B. Davis received special acknowledgment from the town in a grand anniversary ceremony. Parades were held, speeches given, and celebrations ensued. Governor Beauford Jester was on hand as one of the speakers, to pay tribute to Davis's contributions to the oil industry and to the Luling area.[19]

A fitting incident that sets the capstone on Davis's art patronage occurred in 1950, the year before his death, and involves the very first award-winning painting in the Texas Wildflower Competitive Exhibitions—Dawson Dawson-Watson's *The Glory of the Morning*. Back in his flush years, when Davis had presented this winning painting to the Lotus Club of New York City, it had hung in the "social club room" of that organization. When the club disbanded, sometime in the forties, the paintings were sold to art collectors. The particular identity and location of the piece was lost as it passed through the years. Eventually the painting fell into the hands of a South Carolina art dealer who by chance displayed it at an exhibit in San Angelo. There, also by chance, a woman remembered its origin. By the time the news had made its way to friends of Davis, however, the Carolina dealer had already sold the painting to a new owner. Pressed by members of the Luling Foundation board, the dealer was able to negotiate a swap with the painting's new owner, and thus *The Glory of the Morning* was acquired by friends and given as a special gift to Davis. The news accounts reported a "white haired and stooping" Edgar Davis who accepted this special painting with great humility. Then, as would have been his style, he declined to take the painting home to his modest cottage and instead donated it to the Luling Foundation in memory of its trustees and those of the art league who conducted the competition.[20] *The Glory of the Morning* remains there in the offices of the Luling Foundation, a lasting tribute to Edgar Davis's vision and his support of the arts in Texas. That Dawson-Watson's lost masterpiece would somehow find its way back to its aging patron is in many ways exemplary of the mystique that surrounded Davis's artistic interventions. The efforts made by his friends to retrieve this special work for Davis is indicative of the regard and reverence they held for this

The Luling Silver Anniversary Oil Jamboree, August 9, 1947. A community grateful for its prosperity brought about by oil and indebted to its principal oil magnate, Luling celebrated the twenty-fifth anniversary of Davis's discovery well in August of 1947. Here Edgar B. Davis (left) is joined at the jamboree by Magnolia Oil President J. L. Lattimer (center) and Governor Beauford Jester (right). Courtesy Genealogical and Historical Society of Caldwell County

gentleman, who had by then achieved legendary proportions.

Edgar Davis died in 1951 after sustaining a hard fall coming out of his home. He was buried in Luling on October 17 on the grounds of his former home, The House in the Oaks, under a stone that simply acknowledges the spot as the final resting place of "A Man of Faith." In the town, "schools closed, flags flew at half mast, the Texas Lutheran College Choir sang one of Davis's own compositions, 'The Brotherhood of Man.'"[21] Hundreds turned out for the funeral. "Rites were offered by pastors from the Baptist, Christian, Episcopal, Methodist and Presbyterian churches, a priest of the Catholic faith, an elder from the Seventh

Edgar B. Davis in search of new prospects. This photograph depicts Davis (left) with United North and South General Manager Tommy Caylor in about 1950, shortly before Davis's death from a fall. Despite continued litigation and marginal profits for his corporation, Davis continued to drill for oil, confident that his greatest fortune lay deep beneath the Buckeye field on the Texas coast. Courtesy Genealogical and Historical Society of Caldwell County

Day Adventist church and four [black] ministers also helped conduct the services."[22]

Edgar Davis never became president of the United States, as he believed he would. This belief, however, drove Davis's action throughout his lifetime and was never far from his thoughts, even near the end of his life. In late 1949, less than two years before his death,

he wrote to his old friend David Figart, reminding him that "it was forty-five years ago today that I was led to Believe that God had a Mission for me in life and I still Believe that Mission is to be achieved." Who is to say whether Davis misunderstood his message from God, or whether God's plan for him was simply actualized in some other fashion. It is accurate to say,

Scene from Edgar Davis's funeral, 1951. By the time of his death, Davis was revered as a genuine hero in the Luling area. He was a well-loved, first citizen of the area, and his funeral brought many hundreds to pay their last respects. He was buried on the grounds of his former home, The House in the Oaks, in Luling. Courtesy Genealogical and Historical Society of Caldwell County

however, that in his lifetime (at least this particular lifetime) Edgar Davis never achieved the ultimate mantle of leadership he pursued with such great faith and fervor. Nonetheless, it was in the course of these pursuits that Edgar Davis, guided by the hand of God, achieved remarkable things, and in so doing left behind an equally remarkable model of personal faith and corporate virtue.

In his passing Edgar B. Davis did receive the one wish that he had related to his brother Oscar so many years earlier. He effectively died "a poor man," leaving his estate intestate, with every last penny directed to his debtors. His San Antonio attorney Wilbur Mathews later related a story about the time in 1940 when he had broached the subject of a will with his client: "He said that he believed that God would sustain him in continued life and that for him to make a will would be to deny his faith in God. I asked him: 'Do you believe that you are immortal?' He answered with a beatific smile and said: 'Only He knows.' "[23]

With the death of Edgar B. Davis, Texas lost one of its most important personalities of the early century. In addition to his legacy of entrepreneurial success, Edgar Davis left Texans and Americans with a standard of philanthropy and patronage seldom matched since his passing. It has been estimated that Davis gave away over $10,000,000 in his lifetime.[24] Beyond the gifts to his working colleagues and his immediate communities, Davis left a treasure of Texas art that even today memorializes the beauty and richness of the state.

In assessing the Texas Wildflower Competitive Exhibitions, we must conclude that these events that Davis envisioned to repay his debt to the wildflowers now rank among the state's most significant art episodes. Their importance was acknowledged by Texas' earliest art historians, writing during Davis's lifetime. In 1928, Frances Battaile Fisk expressed her view in the first book chronicling art in Texas that "the Wildflower painting contest conducted by the San Antonio Art League . . . has given greater impetus to painting the beauties of the state than any other one thing."[25] Likewise, in Esse Forrester O'Brien's 1935 chronicle of Texas art, she acknowledged the Davis contests as "notable in their encouragement of art in Texas." To O'Brien, this encouragement not only came from the competition's obvious focus on Texas subjects and artists but was also manifested in a healthy rivalry that developed between the state's indigenous painters and those from other locales. In this sense, O'Brien suggests that the contests' larger awards to works by non-Texans served as an impetus for the emerging Texas regionalists (centered primarily in Dallas) to actively promote

and advance their more modern art forms. O'Brien also refers to the contribution the contests made in preserving "many historical scenes, the Texas wildflowers and the life of the South and Southwest in the cotton fields and on the ranches."[26] In her recent biography on the great Texas painter Jerry Bywaters, Francine Carraro describes the competitions among the "sensational" art events of the decade, referencing the national attention the wildflower competitions brought to Texas. She notes that "artists all over Texas were keenly aware of the great interest stirred by the exhibitions and lavish prize money."[27]

It has been written that Edgar B. Davis would do anything to give people happiness and apparently felt that happiness was best achieved in music, in the theater, and in the arts. No doubt Davis himself found great fulfillment in the arts and chose to share this pleasure with others through his varied patronage of the arts. In 1931, Davis himself confirmed his philosophy on this matter in a speech before the San Antonio Women's Club where he stated that "art in all its manifold forms is an attribute of the soul that tends to lift one above the humdrum cares and sordidness of life."[28]

He felt that the pursuit of perfection and ever higher standards in the arts were essential for human progress. Because of his belief in the continuing evolution in the quality and beauty of art forms, Edgar Davis was prone to support the contemporary arts of his time. He was lauded in his lifetime for his active support of living artists, and nowhere was this more apparent than in his design of the Texas Wildflower Competitive Exhibitions. The energy and money he infused into this project presented magnificent and timely encouragement to Texas artists of the day. Yet, with his means and worldly sophistication, Davis might just as easily have directed his attention to the old masters, or perhaps have built an impressive personal collection of works by early American artists. Instead he chose to support local, contemporary artists and their art organizations. His words convey some of his reasons for focusing on the contemporary and provide insights into his optimism for the arts: "It is inconceivable to me that the world's greatest picture has been painted; that the finest statue has been sculpted; that the finest etching has been etched; that the finest wood carving has been carved; that the finest poetry, the finest operas, the finest concertos have been written. Everything about us indicates progress. . . ."[29]

Finally, like John Dewey, Edgar B. Davis felt that art was essential to culture and industry. He stated that "the pursuit of Beauty, which includes progress in the music and the arts, has economic possibilities which are bewildering to the imagination."[30]

Art represented to Edgar B. Davis yet another "road to God," which he pursued with great zeal and enthusiasm.[31] The paintings in the Davis collection remain as perhaps the greatest testament to the inspired vision and artistic philosophy of this great Texan. Today, the Davis collection of the San Antonio Art League sits as one of the undiscovered jewels in the state's modern cultural treasury. The scenes portray the colorful splendor of Texas' natural landscape and celebrate the simple beauties of the state's rural and agrarian past.

Whether by oil or by art, Texas was deeply influenced by the incomparable Edgar B. Davis. His contributions to the state's cultural and economic development in the formative years of the twentieth century cannot be minimized. How fortunate is Texas that its flowers could lift the spirits of a discouraged wildcatter transplanted from Massachusetts via New York, and lead him eventually to the discovery of a great field. How fortunate are we also to be the continuing beneficiaries of Edgar Davis's debt to those wildflowers of Texas.

Plates

Plates of Paintings from the Texas Wildflower Competitive Exhibitions
(Unless otherwise specified, all paintings are in the Davis Collection of the San Antonio Art League.)

1. Dawson Dawson-Watson, The Glory of the Morning

Oil on canvas, 30″ x 40″

National prize, 1927

In the collection of the Luling Foundation, Luling, Texas

2. José Arpa, Verbena
Oil on canvas, 24″ x 34″
Texas prize, 1927

3. Audley Dean Nicols, West Texas Wildflowers

Oil on canvas, 20″ x 30″

Honorable mention, 1927

4. Dawson Dawson-Watson, Spring

Oil on canvas, 30" x 40"

Purchase award, 1927

5. Adrian Brewer, In a Bluebonnet Year

Oil on canvas, 33″ x 36″

First prize, Group 1: Texas Wildflowers (open division), 1928

6. *José Arpa,* Cactus Flowers

Oil on canvas, 30″ x 40″

Third prize, Group 1: Texas Wildflowers (open division), 1928

7. *Henry Keller*, Ranch Life, Western Texas

Oil on canvas, 30″ × 40″

First prize, Group 2: Ranch Life, 1928

8. *Isabel Branson Cartwright,* Cotton Picking Time

Oil on canvas, 30″ x 40″

First prize, Group 3: Cotton Fields, 1928

9. Theodore J. Morgan, Mexican Heather and Salt Cedar

Oil on canvas, 30″ x 35″

First prize, Group 4: Texas Wildflowers (Texas division), 1928

10. Edward G. Eisenlohr, When the Year Is Young

Oil on Canvas, 24″ x 30″

Honorable mention, 1928

11. Rolla Taylor, Blue Fields
Oil on canvas, 24″ x 32″
Honorable mention, 1928

12. Oscar E. Berninghaus, Winter in the Panhandle

Oil on canvas, 30″ x 40″

Honorable mention, 1928

13. W. Herbert Dunton, The Horse Wrangler

Oil on canvas, 25″ x 20″

Honorable mention, 1928

14. Ella K. Mewhinney, Shadows

Oil on canvas, 16" x 20"

Honorable mention, 1928

15. E. Martin Hennings, Thistle Blossoms

Oil on canvas, 30″ x 40″

First prize, Group 1: Texas Wildflowers (open division), 1929

Collection of the Tobin Foundation, Courtesy of the McNay Art Museum, San Antonio

16. Isabel Branson Cartwright, Wild Poppies

Oil on canvas, 30″ x 40″

Fourth prize, Group 1: Texas Wildflowers (open division), 1929

17. Peter Hohnstedt, Evening Shades

Oil on canvas, 37″ x 35″

Fifth prize, Group 1: Texas Wildflowers (open division), 1929

18. Eliot C. Clark, Red-Bud and Wild Plum

Oil on canvas, 30″ x 40″

Seventh prize, Group 1: Texas Wildflowers (open division), 1929

19. Millard Sheets, The Old Goat Ranch

Oil on canvas, 32″ x 36″

Second prize, Group 2: Ranch Life, 1929

20. Frank Tenney Johnson, Texas Night Riders

Oil on canvas, 35" × 40"

Fourth prize, Group 2: Ranch Life, 1929

21. W. Herbert Dunton, Old Texas

Oil on canvas, 28″ x 39″

Fifth prize, Group 2: Ranch Life, 1929

22. José Arpa, Picking Cotton

Oil on canvas, 30″ x 40″

First prize, Group 3: Cotton Fields, 1929

23. Oscar E. Berninghaus, Cotton Picking
Oil on canvas, 30″ x 40″
Second prize, Group 3: Cotton Fields, 1929

24. Louis Raynaud, Picaninnies in Cotton

Oil on canvas, 34″ x 39″

Third prize, Group 3: Cotton Fields, 1929

25. Dawson Dawson-Watson, Early Morning

Oil on canvas, 30″ x 40″

Fifth prize, Group 3: Cotton Fields, 1929

26. Dawson Dawson-Watson, The Bouquet

Oil on canvas, 30" x 40"

First prize, Group 4: Texas Wildflowers (Texas division), 1929

27. Peter Hohnstedt, Sunshine and Shadow

Oil on canvas, 29″ x 35″

Second prize, Group 4: Texas Wildflowers (Texas division), 1929

28. Ella K. Mewhinney, Texas Wild Flowers

Oil on canvas, 30″ x 26″

Third prize, Group 4: Texas Wildflowers (Texas division), 1929

29. *Xavier Gonzalez, Twilight*

Oil on canvas, 30″ x 40″

Purchase prize, San Antonio Art League, 1929

Afterword

It is always a labor of love to work with the Davis competitions' paintings in the collection of the San Antonio Art League. This collection is unique in that it represents the best of artistic production in the state of Texas for a very limited period, 1927–29. Yet, these few works show the endless variety of the Texas landscape and atmosphere that those of us who live here appreciate and respect.

In the Davis paintings the viewer is treated to the ever-changing Texas sky, sometimes blue, sometimes gray, sometimes clear, and sometimes cloudy, but always grand. Like the sky, the land too is always grand, whether it be the Hill Country of Central Texas, the beautiful Coastal Bend, the flat and endless northern plains, or the rugged West Texas deserts. With the Davis paintings, we are treated to all these areas in a variety of conditions. Hot and dry or hot and humid, air so clear you can see forever or so laden with moisture you feel as if you should swim—all of this is illustrated in these great works of art.

Following are some of my impressions of these paintings. This is not meant to be an art historical overview of the artists and the works. Rather, I hope these few comments will encourage you to look at the paintings carefully and to get your own message from them. I hope you will walk away from each work saying, "I've been there and I've seen that."

RICHARD CASAGRANDE
Board of Directors, San Antonio Art League

JOSÉ ARPA (1858–1952)

José Arpa is the most international of the Davis competitions' artists. Beginning and ending his career in Spain, Arpa was brought to Mexico by the Mexican government in the 1890s to teach art, and he soon settled in San Antonio, where he painted many of his greatest landscapes.

Verbena (plate 2), with its sweep of pink and its

strong diagonal lines, creates an exquisite harmony of color and line. The painting stands as a monument to Texas wildflower art and forms a fine contrast to the numerous bluebonnet scenes in the art league's collection.

Cactus Flowers (plate 6), like *Verbena,* is painted with a diagonal axis, which encourages the eye to continually move throughout the composition. In the distance we see cliffs of the Texas Hill Country, and Arpa employs one of his favorite compositional elements, a strong horizontal horizon. In all of Arpa's paintings in the Davis Collection, we see a clarity of atmosphere, which is the artist's hallmark and a reminder of his Spanish art education.

In the 1929 painting, *Picking Cotton* (plate 22), Arpa has introduced the human element. The portrait of the young boy in the foreground makes a social statement that is as relevant today as it was in 1929. The toil of working in the hot fields is vividly intensified by the shimmering light and the weight of the distant horizontal horizon.

OSCAR E. BERNINGHAUS (1874–1952)
Berninghaus is definitely not a Texas Hill Country painter. His two works in the Davis Collection show the endless flat horizon of the Great Plains and are wonderful contrasts to the numerous Hill Country images. Berninghaus was a founding member of the Taos Society of Artists and was mainly self-taught. He apprenticed as a printer, where he learned to draw and to work with color, lessons that would later be translated into his well-executed and gently colored landscapes.

Winter in the Panhandle (plate 12) is the only work from the 1928 competition to depict a winter scene. Painted mainly in whites and grays, the landscape, buildings, and sky are all frozen in place. Even the cattle are unmoving, for the moment. The painting has elegant compositional elements, the barbed wire fence drawing the viewer's eye to the snow-blanketed buildings, which are all dwarfed by the expanse of the vast Texas sky.

Cotton Picking (plate 23) portrays the same Texas landscape after it has awakened from the winter cold and is now bathed in light partially obscured by big, billowing clouds. The clouds do not give hope for relief from the heat, just as the gray sky in *Winter in the Panhandle* does not foreshadow relief from the cold. Unlike the other paintings of cotton picking in the collection, Berninghaus chose to show the great expanse of the Texas landscape, while the numerous figures and animals and the wagon create a panorama typical of the artist's works.

ADRIAN BREWER (1891–1957)
This work is most typical of what one expects to see in a Texas Hill Country landscape. *In a Bluebonnet Year* (plate 5) depicts the best of bluebonnet paintings with the soft expanse of blue in the painting contrasted with the Texas sunlight in the middle and distant landscape.

ISABEL B. CARTWRIGHT (1885–1966)
Isabel Cartwright was originally from Philadelphia and was best known as a portrait artist. *Cotton Picking Time* (plate 8) is similar in subject and imagery to Arpa's

and Dawson-Watson's paintings without the sophistication of these two. Cartwright has abstracted the image, creating broad blocks and patches of color. Although proficient, the piece lacks the originality and strength of its two companion pieces. As Cartwright was primarily a portrait painter, the greatest strength of the picture is the image of the young boy in the upper right corner. The direct eye contact of the boy with the viewer draws us into the composition and forces us to interact with what otherwise might be a vapid image.

Wild Poppies (plate 16), however, illustrates the imagination and creativity of the artist better than *Cotton Picking Time.* In this work, Cartwright has magnified the poppy flowers and given them a presence deserving of their beauty. The contrasts of light and shade, bright hues, and shadow imbue the work with a freshness that stands alone in the 1929 Davis competition paintings.

ELIOT C. CLARK (1883–19?)

Red-Bud and Wild Plum (plate 18) is not a typical wildflower painting, in that we see trees in bloom and beautiful white and pinks, while the earth is still brown from the winter chill. Clark carries the colors of the midground trees into the background with faint touches of color. The painting is particularly interesting because one does not usually think of blossoming trees as wildflowers.

DAWSON DAWSON-WATSON (1864–1939)

Dawson Dawson-Watson had achieved prominent stature as an artist long before moving to San Antonio in 1927. He painted in the Midwest, and works from that area are sought after. After moving to San Antonio, Dawson-Watson became the area's most renowned cactus painter.

Spring (plate 4) is a beautiful landscape of the Texas Hill Country depicting a vista of fields, trees, and rolling hills. The presentation of the scene is more atmospheric than the paintings of José Arpa, as the air seems to be laden with moisture. Dawson-Watson is a master in his application of paint, and his splashes of color give a spontaneity and depth that is strictly his own. Dawson-Watson's paintings have a slightly blurry quality, which creates a subtle sense of shimmer and movement.

Early Morning (plate 25) illustrates the same theme as Arpa's *Picking Cotton* from a completely different point of view. While Arpa's painting moves toward the viewer, Dawson-Watson's takes us away from the foreground, which is accentuated by the worm's eye view, the diagonal recession of the figures and the strong atmospheric perspective. The figures are lost in their own thoughts, and the viewer is not invited to participate.

Impressionistic is the only way to describe *The Bouquet* (plate 26). In this painting the light shines as Dawson-Watson brings the beauty of the cactus flower into our presence by the immediacy of the image. The misty background of the painting and the slightly blurred image allow the landscape to emerge from the background in a ghostlike way.

W. HERBERT DUNTON (1878–1936)

Dunton is probably one of the best known artists in the Davis Collection, due in part to the popularity of Western painting and in part to the excellence of the artist's work. Like Berninghaus, Dunton was a founding member of the Taos Society of Artists. He worked for many years as an illustrator and continued the genre of Remington and Russell. He spent time as a cow-puncher and, in order to assure accuracy in his art, drew in the field. Dunton brings the art of the cowboy artist into the twentieth century through his illustrative style and composition.

The Horse Wrangler (plate 13) shows the vast panorama of West Texas as does Berninghaus's works. However, unlike Berninghaus, the artist has ennobled the cowhand by his prominent placement in the entire foreground of the piece. His gaze over his shoulder draws the viewer's attention to the activities in the background of the painting, while the turbulence of the cloudy sky drapes the work with a majestic backdrop.

Old Texas (plate 21) again shows the artist's ability to draw the viewer into the painting by creating a strong single-point perspective through which the flowing river, the agitated longhorn cattle, and the horse and cowboy must maneuver. In this instance, Dunton has draped the background with low rolling hills below a dark and ominous sky. Dunton is one of the most painterly artists in the collection, and *Old Texas* and *The Horse Wrangler* emphasize the artist's mastery of the brush, although he never abandons the illustrator's outline.

EDWARD G. EISENLOHR (1872–1961)

Eisenlohr, like W. Herbert Dunton, paints with a broader brush than some of the painters in the Davis Collection. The artist was a student of two prominent Texas painters, Robert Onderdonk and Frank Reaugh. Both artists were impressionistic in their overall style, and this influence is seen in Eisenlohr's painting *When the Year Is Young* (plate 10). The artist uses warm hues in his composition, with solid strong brush strokes to depict this springtime landscape.

XAVIER GONZALEZ (1898–1993)

Xavier Gonzalez was the nephew of José Arpa and came to San Antonio in the 1920s to assist his uncle as an art instructor. Of all the works in the Davis Collection, *Twilight* (plate 29) is probably the most powerful. The figures' heads are bowed and it is up to the viewer to determine if in prayer or despair. The theme of cotton picking becomes trivial next to the power of the image and the spiritual overtones portrayed in this work.

PETER HOHENSTEDT (1872–1957)

Hohenstedt's favorite color must have been turquoise, as it is seen in nearly all of his compositions. *Evening Shades* (plate 17) is somewhat impressionistic; the strongly shadowed foreground is painted in deep blue, while the valley and mountains in the background are saturated with light, allowing the artist to use his typical pastel palette and turquoise coloration.

Sunshine and Shadow (plate 27) is meant to be viewed from a distance. Unlike *Evening Shades*, the artist has separated colors with rather large brush strokes, which, when viewed up close, segment the painted surface. When the viewer steps back, the colors blend to create beautiful tonal gradations and great depth of perspective.

FRANK TENNEY JOHNSON (1874–1939)

The painting *Texas Night Riders* (plate 20) by Johnson is one of the most dramatic in the collection and is a rarely seen night view of Texas ranch life. Johnson, like Dunton, paints in the tradition of Remington and illustrates ranch life from the point of view of the traditional cowboy. This painting is particularly striking because of the overall green tonality and the wonderful starlit sky.

HENRY KELLER (1870–1949)

Ranch Life, Western Texas (plate 7) depicts cowboy life in the 1920s. Keller, unlike many of the other artists in the Davis Collection, has stylized the images to create a patchwork picture. We see strong movement to the right and left of the composition, all of which is dissected by the vertical lines of the trees and the horizontal bands of the land and river. The image is of a thick, lush, and nearly abstract landscape, the trees heavy with leaf as they shade the cowboys and cattle.

ELLA K. MEWHINNEY (1891–19?)

Mewhinney's painting *Shadows* (plate 14) repeats some of the compositional elements seen in Keller's *Ranch Life, Western Texas,* with the strong verticals depicted in the trees dissected by the horizontal bands of the landscape. Unlike Keller, Mewhinney has not abstracted the painted plane, although the technique is strongly impressionistic. She has also chosen to contrast the impressionistic brushwork of the wildflowers with the strong solid lines of the sinuous and somewhat unnatural curves of the trees.

  Texas Wild Flowers (plate 28) is the only still-life painting in the collection. The artist chose to show the flowers arranged in a vase sitting on a window ledge backed by a white curtain with shadows of a window frame. The flowers are depicted in a painterly manner, which is juxtaposed with the careful arrangement of the painted elements.

THEODORE J. MORGAN (1872–19?)

In *Mexican Heather and Salt Cedar* (plate 9), Morgan takes the viewer to another part of Texas—the Gulf Coast. The artist chose a pastel palette to depict the expanse of heather, while a solitary clump of salt cedar balances the distant seascape and sun-drenched sky. Unlike many paintings in the collection, the artist chose to portray the atmosphere as a hazy screen through which the flowers and forms emerge. There is little detail in this work, unlike many of the other landscapes, and the piece is in sharp contrast to the atmospheric clarity of Arpa's and Nicols's works.

AUDLEY DEAN NICOLS (1874–1941)

Nicols's painting *West Texas Wildflowers* (plate 3) is unique to the 1927 Davis competition paintings in that it illustrates as a pure landscape the expansive desert and barren mountains of West Texas. The perspective of the vanishing road and the endless horizon creates a vista unlike the other landscapes in the collection. This painting requires close scrutiny to discover the lushness of the land depicted in detail in the foreground, while the background and overall tonality of the work reveal the dry heat in which West Texas wildflowers thrive.

LOUIS RAYNAUD (18? –19?)

Picaninnies in Cotton (plate 24) is not a "politically correct" painting by today's standards and must be viewed as a work of its time. The artist has chosen to portray the stereotypical image of the African-American fieldworker, with almost doll-like little girls in the foreground. Although the artist is competent, there is almost a folk-art quality to this painting, which gives it charm rather than presence.

MILLARD SHEETS (1907–)

Millard Sheets was a promising artist at the age of twenty-one when he executed the work *The Old Goat Ranch* (plate 19). The prize moneys from the 1929 Davis competition allowed the artist to make a year-long trip to Europe to further his painting education. This work is painted with strong brushwork and powerful colors. The numerous activities in the canvas, as well as the imagery, require the viewer to examine its many elements to see how it is painted and what is depicted. This image of ranch life is quite different from any of the other works in the collection in that there is an intimacy in the overall image rather than an illustration of the expanse of the Texas scene.

ROLLA TAYLOR (1872–1970)

Rolla Taylor was truly a "Sunday painter," working as a court reporter in Bexar County for more than fifty years. The landscape work in the Davis Collection, *Blue Fields* (plate 11), is an unusual work in the artist's genre in that it isn't the typical urban scene. The painting is, in fact, one of the artist's greatest and most accomplished works. Taylor used the muted tones of his early palette, which was replaced in later years with brighter colors. The painting, unlike the other bluebonnet works in the collection, is rather somber and dark, which provides a different perspective of the Texas Hill Country landscape.

Appendix

Texas Wildflower Competitive Exhibitions, Winners and Entrants

Paintings marked "Davis" can be found in the Davis Collection of the San Antonio Art League. Those marked "Luling" are in the collection of the Luling Foundation, Luling, Texas, while those marked "McNay" are located in the McNay Museum, San Antonio, Texas.

1927

Awards

NATIONAL PRIZE
Dawson Dawson-Watson,
The Glory of the Morning [Luling]

TEXAS PRIZE
José Arpa,
Verbena [Davis]

Entrants

NATIONAL PRIZE
Arpa, José; San Antonio, Texas
Bandera Road
Bluebonnets

Braun, Maurice; Point Loma, California
Live Oaks and Bluebonnets
Vista on Babcock Road

Brewer, Adrian; Little Rock, Arkansas
Bluebonnet Field in Texas
Evening in Bluebonnet Country
Spring Morning in Texas

Brewer, Nicholas R.; Little Rock, Arkansas
Bluebonnet Field
The Carpeted Hillside
Spring in Texas

Bryan, W. Edward; Dublin, Texas
Texas Wild Verbena

Castleden, George F.; New Orleans, Louisiana
Bird Nest Hunters

Cherry, Emma Richardson; Houston, Texas
Texas Landscape with Wild Flowers—Near Austin

Crews, Seth Floyd, Jr.; El Paso, Texas
Cooper Mallow

Cuprien, F. W.; Laguna Beach, California
Texas Bluebonnets

Dawson-Watson, Dawson; Saint Louis, Missouri
Flowers of the Field
The Glory of the Morning [Luling]
Spring [Davis]

Eisenlohr, Edward G.; Dallas, Texas
Spring Fields at Grand Prairie

Gamble, John M.; Santa Barbara, California
Bluebonnets
Spring Flowers

Gideon, Samuel E.; Austin, Texas
Coryopsis Time in Texas

Gonzales, Boyer; Galveston, Texas
Where the Blue Begins

Hogue, Alexandre; Dallas, Texas
Bear Grass

Huddle, Nannie; Austin, Texas
Bluebonnets

Hull, Marie A.; Jackson, Mississippi
Bluebonnets
Spring in Texas

McGill, Eloise Polk; San Antonio, Texas
The Year's at Spring

Morgan, Theodore J.; San Diego, California
Desert Trail
The Soul of Texas

Nave, Royston; Victoria, Texas
Texas Wildflowers

Shuhart, Donald Vincent; Stillwater, Oklahoma
Tokens of Texas

Taylor, Rolla; San Antonio, Texas
Blue and Gold [Davis]

Wilkinson, Edward; Houston, Texas
Where Many a Flower Grows Wild

TEXAS PRIZE

Allen, Clarence; San Antonio
A Field of Blue

Arpa, José; San Antonio
Verbena [Davis]

Bell, Mrs. A. J.; San Antonio
A Cloudy Day

Brockman, Marie; Mason
Bluebonnets

Bryan, W. Edward; Dublin
Blue Bonnet Hills

Cherry, Emma Richardson; Houston
Texas Landscape with Wild Flowers—Wine Cups

Coleman, Mrs. W. P.; San Antonio
Spring in Texas

Cook, Paul Rodda, Jr.; San Antonio
Bluebonnets at Morning

Crocker, Edna Earl; San Antonio
When Texas Was in Flower

Crowther, Mollie L.; San Angelo
A Glorious Morning

Downie, Janet; Austin
Bluebonnet Valley

Emeree, Berla Iyone; El Paso
Bluebonnets of Helotes

Enser, John. F.; San Antonio
Bluebonnets and Verbenas

Everett, Raymond; Austin
Cloudy Sunrise

Fletcher, Vallie; Beaumont
Bluebonnets

Foster, M.; Houston
The Magic Carpet of Texas

Fowler, Eva; Sherman
Dandelions

Gideon, Samuel E.; Austin
Firewheels and Thistles

Gordon, Clara F.; San Antonio
Roadside Glory

Hardin, Ernest R.; Georgetown
The Blue Dale

Harpham, Carolyn Rose; San Antonio
Verbenas

Hellman, Bertha Louise; Houston
Clothier's Place—Ft. Davis

Huddle, Nannie; Austin
Early Spring

Jackson, Everett Gee; Mexia
Bluebonnets of Tehuacona Hills

King, Gillis; Austin
Fields of Gold

Leberman, Virginia; Austin
Bluebonnets in Travis Heights

McGill, Eloise Polk; San Antonio
Glory in the Flower

Mewhinney, Ella K.; Holland
Blue and Gold

Moseley, Nell; Fort Worth
Texas Oaks and Flowers

Nave, Royston; Victoria
Victoria Wildflowers

Neumann, Gilbert; San Antonio
Landscape, Texas

Nicols, Audley Dean; El Paso
West Texas Wildflowers

Palmer, Jesse; Amarillo
Spring Time near Dallas

Smith, Alexa; San Antonio
Foot Hills of Texas

Taylor, Rolla; San Antonio
Evening

Thurston, Eugene; El Paso
Desert Gold

Tupper, Margaret W.; San Antonio
Texas Fields

Walker, Mrs. Wm. Phillip; San Antonio
Spring Time at Elmendorf

Wansley, Kate; Fort Worth
Blue and Gold

Weisser, Mrs. Fred W.; San Antonio
Texas Wildflowers

Wheeler, Ellie; San Antonio
Texas Wildflowers

Wilkinson, Edward; Houston
By the Side of the Road

1928

Awards

GROUP 1: TEXAS WILDFLOWERS
(OPEN DIVISION)

1. Adrian Brewer, *In a Bluebonnet Year* [Davis]
2. William Silva, *Wild Poppies on the Creek Bank*
3. José Arpa, *Cactus Flowers* [Davis]
4. Benjamin Brown, *When Bluebonnets Bloom*

GROUP 2: RANCH LIFE

1. Henry Keller, *Ranch Life, Western Texas* [Davis]
2. Power O'Malley, *Evening on X Ranch, Texas*

GROUP 3: COTTON FIELDS

1. Isabel Branson Cartwright, *Cotton Picking Time* [Davis]
2. T. Lawson Blackmon, *Sunny Afternoon*

GROUP 4: TEXAS WILDFLOWERS
(TEXAS DIVISION)

1. Theodore J. Morgan, *Mexican Heather and Salt Cedar* [Davis]
2. Audley Dean Nicols, *Texas Plains*

Entrants

GROUP 1: TEXAS WILDFLOWERS

Arpa, José; San Antonio, Texas
Cactus Flowers [Davis]

Birren, Joseph; Chicago, Illinois
Floral Glory of Palo Duro Canyon

Blackmon, T. Lawson; San Antonio, Texas
Wine Cups

Brewer, Adrian; Little Rock, Arkansas
In a Bluebonnet Year [Davis]

Brown, Benjamin C.; Pasadena, California
When Bluebonnets Bloom

Cook, Paul Rodda, Jr.; San Antonio, Texas
Spring Day

Crews, Seth Floyd, Jr.; El Paso, Texas
Early Morning

Crocker, Edna Earl; San Antonio, Texas
Morning with the Flowers

Dawson-Watson, Dawson; San Antonio, Texas
Flowers of Silk
The Gold That Is Texas

Dunbier, Augustus H.; Omaha, Nebraska
Roadside Wild-Life

Edstrom, Miriam I.; San Antonio, Texas
When the Cactus Is Decorative

Eisenlohr, Edward G.; Dallas, Texas
When the Year Is Young [Davis]

Griffith, Louis O.; Nashville, Indiana
Spring's Enchantment

Haines, Marie; College Station, Texas
Rose-Clad Hills (Texas Star)

Jackson, Everett Gee; Mexia, Texas
Wild Flowers in Abbie's Yard

Mewhinney, Ella K.; Holland, Texas
Niggerheads

Morgan, Theodore J.; San Antonio, Texas
Morning near Bandera
Vista from Droughtfels

Nichols, Mary Roberta; El Paso, Texas
The Golden Stairway

Page, Harvey L.; Alamo Heights, Texas
Sunset, Alamo Valley

Pancoast, Clara Caffrey; San Antonio, Texas
Boerne Mountain Pinks

Silva, William P.; Carmel, California
Wild Poppies on the Creek Bank

Taylor, Rolla; San Antonio, Texas
Blue Fields [Davis]

Teel, Lewis W.; El Paso, Texas
Western Trail

Tompsett, Ruth R.; Omaha, Nebraska
Texas Sunshine

Wilkinson, Edward; Houston, Texas
Golden Spring

Woeffle, Arthur W.; Flushing, New York
Flower, Still Life

GROUP 2: RANCH LIFE

Berninghaus, Oscar E.; Taos, New Mexico
Winter in the Panhandle [Davis]

Brewer, Adrian; Little Rock, Arkansas
Daisies on Fredericksburg Road

Cartwright, Isabel Branson; Philadelphia, Pennsylvania
At the Corral

Cherry, Emma Richardson; Houston, Texas
Ranch Life

Cook, Paul Rodda, Jr.; San Antonio, Texas
Night in the Boerne Hill

Crews, Seth Floyd, Jr.; El Paso, Texas
Bringing in the Strays

Davidson, McNeill; Houston, Texas
The Hog Wallow

Diaz, Emilio G.; San Antonio, Texas
Dawn in the Ranch

Dunton, W. Herbert; Taos, New Mexico
The Horse Wrangler [Davis]
The Trail Boss

Edstrom, Miriam I.; San Antonio, Texas
Before Breakfast
Roping the Horses

Eisenlohr, Edward G.; Dallas, Texas
The Passing of the Ranch

Emeree, Berla Iyone; El Paso, Texas
West Texas Ranch Life

Gonzales, Boyer; Galveston, Texas
The Passing Herd

Hull, Marie A.; Jackson, Mississippi
Evening on the Ranch—Texas

Keller, Henry G.; Cleveland, Ohio
Ranch Life, Western Texas [Davis]

McGill, Eloise Polk; San Antonio, Texas
Out Where the West Begins

Morgan, Theodore J.; San Antonio, Texas
In the Big Bend Country

Nave, Royston; Victoria, Texas
Fence Corner

O'Malley, Power; Los Angeles, California
Afternoon, X Ranch, Texas
Evening on X Ranch, Texas

Schlichting, H. C.; Darien, Connecticut
Rounding Them Up

Taylor, Rolla; San Antonio
The Cabin

Tupper, Margaret Wright; San Antonio, Texas
The Texas Range

Walker, Mrs. Wm. Phillip; San Antonio, Texas
Ranch Scene near San Antonio

Williams, Howe; Tempe, Arizona
Barnyard Friends

Workman, David T.; Minneapolis, Minnesota
The Last Load

GROUP 3: COTTON FIELDS

Altheide, Harvi C.; San Antonio, Texas
King Cotton

Arpa, José; San Antonio, Texas
Cotton Pickers

Blackmon, T. Lawson; San Antonio, Texas
Out Early
Sunny Afternoon

Cartwright, Isabel Branson; Philadelphia, Pennsylvania
Cotton Picking Time [Davis]

Dawson-Watson, Dawson; San Antonio, Texas
Cotton Field—Morning
The Cotton Picker

Eisenlohr, Edward G.; Dallas, Texas
When Cotton Fields Are Brown

Gideon, Samuel E.; Austin, Texas
Under Texas Skies

Hull, Marie A.; Jackson, Mississippi
The Cotton Pickers

Jackson, Everett Gee; Mexia, Texas
Scrapping Up
To Pick the Top Crop

McLeary, Kindred; Austin, Texas
Cotton

Mewhinney, Ella K.; Holland, Texas
Gleaners of the South
In the Land of Cotton

Morgan, Theodore J.; San Antonio, Texas
The Row Road

Myers, Edmund D.; Wilmington, Delaware
The Old and New

Shuhart, Donald Vincent; Stillwater, Oklahoma
Near the End of the Row

GROUP 4: TEXAS WILDFLOWERS

Bell, Mrs. A. J.; San Antonio
In Springtime

Bryan, W. Edward; Dublin
Sun Flowers

Christianson, Carl; Austin
Texas Prairie Flowers

Collins, Edna; Austin
Bright Horizons

Dawson-Watson, Dawson; San Antonio
Dawn

Eisenlohr, Edward G.; Dallas
Pasture in Spring

Gideon, Samuel E.; Austin
Field of Mountain Pink

Gudger, Muriel Ruth; El Paso
Texas Wildflowers

Jackson, Everett Gee; Mexia
The Last Flowers and Leaves

Kinney, Mrs. John U.; San Antonio
Old-Fashioned Bouquet of Texas Wildflowers

Mewhinney, Ella K.; Holland
Shadows [Davis]

Morgan, Theodore J.; San Antonio
Coreopsis near Leon Springs
Mexican Heather and Salt Cedar [Davis]

Nicols, Audley Dean; El Paso
Texas Plains
West Texas Wild Flowers

Spellman, Coreen Mary; Denton
Morning Glows

Teel, Lewis W.; El Paso
Desert Carpet

Weisser, Mrs. Fred W.; San Antonio
Texas Wild Flower Scene

Wood, Robert; San Antonio
Spanish Dagger

1929

Awards

GROUP 1: TEXAS WILDFLOWERS
(OPEN DIVISION)
1. E. Martin Hennings, *Thistle Blossoms* [McNay]
2. Marie Hull, *Texas Field Flowers*
3. Maurice Braun, *Texas Fields*
4. Isabel Branson Cartwright, *Wild Poppies* [Davis]
5. Peter L. Hohnstedt, *Evening Shades* [Davis]
6. Louis O. Griffith, *Tranquil Afternoon*
7. Eliot Clark, *Red-Bud and Wild Plum* [Davis]

GROUP 2: RANCH LIFE
1. Glenn Newell, *Upper Range*
2. Millard Sheets, *The Old Goat Ranch* [Davis]
3. O. E. Berninghaus, *Peaceful Life on the Ranch*
4. Frank Tenney Johnson, *Texas Night Riders* [Davis]
5. W. Herbert Dunton, *Old Texas* [Davis]

GROUP 3: COTTON FIELDS
1. José Arpa, *Picking Cotton* [Davis]
2. Oscar E. Berninghaus, *Cotton Picking* [Davis]

3. Louis Raynaud, *Picaninnies in Cotton* [Davis]
4. Nicholas Brewer, *The Cotton Harvest*
5. Dawson Dawson-Watson, *Early Morning* [Davis]

GROUP 4: TEXAS WILDFLOWERS
(TEXAS DIVISION)
1. Dawson Dawson-Watson, *The Bouquet* [Davis]
2. P. L. Hohnstedt, *Sunshine and Shadow* [Davis]
3. Ella K. Mewhinney, *Texas Wild Flowers* [Davis]
4. Jessiejo Eckford, *Prickly Pear*

Entrants

GROUP 1: TEXAS WILDFLOWERS
Bachofen, Max Albin; Castroville, Texas
A Fall Flower

Bell, Mrs. A. J.; San Antonio, Texas
By the Roadside

Braun, Maurice; Point Loma, California
Texas Fields

Brewer, Adrian; Little Rock, Arkansas
Lowland Bluebonnets at Sunset
Verbena in Sandy Hills

Burgdorft, Ferdinand; Pebble Beach, California
A Texas Pot of Gold

Cartwright, Isabel Branson; Philadelphia, Pennsylvania
El Nopal
Wild Poppies [Davis]

Clark, Eliot; New York City, New York
Red-Bud and Wild Plum [Davis]

Cook, Paul Rodda, Jr.; San Antonio, Texas
The Last of the Summer Flowers
Spring in the Hill Country

Cosgrove, Suzanna; San Antonio, Texas
Cactus

Critcher, Catherine; Washington, D.C.
Texas Cacti

Cronin, Marie; Bartlett, Texas
Field Flowers, Llano County

Dawson-Watson, Dawson; San Antonio, Texas
Solomon in All His Glory Was Not Arrayed
Like One of These

Desplats, Denise; Corpus Christi, Texas
Still Life Wild Flowers

DeYoung, Harry Anthony; San Antonio, Texas
Autumn Gold
When November Fields Are Yellow

Doke, Mrs. Fred; Shreveport, Louisiana
The Pewter Pitcher

Edwards, Emily; Matamoros, Mexico
Prickly Pear

Eisenlohr, Edward G.; Dallas, Texas
Fields in May
On the Fredericksburg Road

Gonzalez, Xavier; San Antonio, Texas
Spring in Texas

Griffith, Louis O.; Nashville, Indiana
Fertile Fields
Tranquil Afternoon

Griffith, William A.; Laguna Beach, California
April
Home Glorified

Blackmon, T. Lawson; San Antonio, Texas
Weighing Up

Bradshaw, Alexandra; Fresno, California
Land of Cotton

Brewer, Nicholas R.; Little Rock, Arkansas
The Cotton Harvest

Dawson-Watson, Dawson; San Antonio, Texas
Early Morning [Davis]

Enser, John F.; San Antonio, Texas
Cotton Pickers

Goldthwaite, Anne; New York City, New York
Cotton Fields in August
Cotton Picking Time

Gonzalez, Xavier; San Antonio, Texas
Twilight [Davis]

Heldner, Knute; New Orleans, Louisiana
In the Cotton Field

Hull, Marie A.; Jackson, Mississippi
Bent Backs of the Cotton Field

Jackson, Everett Gee; San Diego, California
Cotton Pickers, East Texas

Keller, Henry G.; Cleveland, Ohio
Irrigating Cotton Fields along the Rio Grande

Klepper, Frank; Dallas, Texas
Last Bale

Knecht, Fern Edie; Little Rock, Arkansas
A Sunny Day

McLellan, Ralph; Philadelphia, Pennsylvania
Hoeing Cotton

Millet, Clarence; New Orleans, Louisiana
Louisiana Cotton Fields
Picking Cotton

Moen, Ella C.; Fresno, California
In the Cotton Fields

Morgan, Theodore J.; Castroville, Texas
The Back Country

Raynaud, Louis; New Orleans, Louisiana
Picaninnies in Cotton [Davis]

Rutland, Emily; San Antonio, Texas
Cotton Harvest

Saunders, L. Pearl; Jackson, Tennessee
Weighing Cotton

Sheets, Millard Owen; Hollywood, California
Loading Cotton

Tracy, Helise; Castroville, Texas
The Cotton Grower's Dream

Ward, J. Stephen; Oklahoma City, Oklahoma
When Harvest Days Are Over

Wood, Virginia H.; Albermarle County, Virginia
Ending the Day

GROUP 4: TEXAS WILDFLOWERS

Bell, Mrs. A. J.; San Antonio
Midsummer

Cook, Paul Rodda, Jr.; San Antonio
Hillside

Crews, Seth Floyd, Jr.; El Paso
A Hill of Blue

Crocker, Edna Earl; San Antonio
Wildflowers

Dawson-Watson, Dawson; San Antonio
The Bouquet [Davis]

Dawson-Watson, Edward; San Antonio
Texas Beauties

Eckford, Jessiejo; Dallas
Prickly Pear

Eisenlohr, Edward G.; Dallas
May Morning
The Mottled Field

Enser, John F.; San Antonio
Horse Mint Field

Gonzalez, Xavier; San Antonio
Somewhere in Texas

Haines, Marie; College Station
East Texas Bluebells

Harpham, Carolyn Rose; San Antonio
Verbenas

Hohnstedt, Peter L.; San Antonio
Sunny Hillside
Sunshine and Shadow [Davis]

Klepper, Frank; Dallas
Texas Plumes

Mewhinney, Ella K.; Holland
Texas Wild Flowers [Davis]

Morgan, Theodore J.; Castroville
Early Morning (Mountain Pink and Mesquite)

Pancoast, Clara Caffrey; San Antonio
Hill Side Flowers

Reeves, Charlotte; San Antonio
Bluebonnets
Landscape

Spellman, Coreen Mary; East Orange, New Jersey
Sunflowers

Tracy, Helise; Castroville
Huisache Tree

Walker, Mrs. Wm. Phillip; Luling
Dust of Gold

Weisser, Mrs. Fred W.; San Antonio
Bluebonnets

Notes

CHAPTER I.
AN INTRODUCTION AND BACKDROP

1. Riley Froh, "The Folklore and Facts behind the Luling Discovery Well," *Plum Creek Almanac* 2, no. 2 (Fall, 1984): 90.

2. Marie Seacord Lilly, "The Texas Wild Flower Painting Competitions," *American Magazine of Art* XX (June, 1929): 342.

3. Ibid.

4. Jerry Bywaters, "Introduction," in *Painting in Texas: The Nineteenth Century*, by Pauline A. Pinckney, p. XVII.

5. Goetzmann, William H., "Introduction," in *Art for History's Sake: The Texas Collection of the Witte Museum*, by Cecilia Steinfeldt, p. XIX.

6. Esse Forrester O'Brien, *Art and Artists of Texas*, p. 4.

7. Sam Deshong Ratcliffe, *Painting Texas History to 1900*, pp. 10–14.

8. Bywaters, "Introduction," in *Painting in Texas*, by Pinckney, p. XVIII.

9. Frances Battaile Fisk, *A History of Texas Artists and Sculptors*, p. 4.

10. William H. Goetzmann and William N. Goetzmann, *The West of the Imagination*, pp. 83–85.

11. Steinfeldt, *Art for History's Sake*, pp. 59–61, 238–45.

12. Cecilia Steinfeldt, *The Onderdonks: A Family of Texas Painters*, p. 17.

13. Ibid., p. 20.

14. Francine Carraro, *Jerry Bywaters: A Life in Art*, p. 11.

15. Steinfeldt, *The Onderdonks*, p. 14.

16. Fisk, *A History of Texas Artists and Sculptors*, pp. 4–5.

17. William J. Battle, "Art in Texas: An Outline," *Southwest Review* XIV, no. 1 (Autumn, 1928): 58.

18. Marion Murray, "Art in the Southwest," *Southwest Review* 12, no. 4 (July, 1926): 290.

19. Fisk, *A History of Texas Artists and Sculptors*, pp. 177–78.

20. Carraro, *Jerry Bywaters*, p. 38.

21. Susan Landauer and Becky Duval Reese, "Lone Star Spirits," in *Independent Spirits: Women Painters of the American West, 1890–1945*, ed. Patricia Trenton, p. 183.

22. Murray, "Art in the Southwest," pp. 289–90.

23. Fisk, *A History of Texas Artists and Sculptors*, p. 4.

24. Cecilia Steinfeldt, "Blooming Bluebonnets: A Texas Tradition," *Southwest Art* 14 (Apr., 1985): 66.

25. Battle, "Art in Texas," p. 57.

26. Susie Kalil, *The Texas Landscape, 1900–1986*, p. 21.

27. Ibid., p. 30.

28. Riley Froh, *Edgar B. Davis: Wildcatter Extraordinary*, p. 43.

29. Wilbur L. Matthews, *San Antonio Lawyer: Memoranda of Cases and Clients*, p. 117.

CHAPTER 2.
A MAN OF FAITH
AND A MAN OF VISION

1. Lincoln K. Davis, *Edgar B. Davis: A Native Son Who Never Forgot His Home Town*, p. 1.
2. Riley Froh, *Edgar B. Davis and Sequences in Business Capitalism: From Shoes to Rubber to Oil*, pp. 4, 22.
3. Ibid., pp. 7, 9.
4. Murdock Pemberton, "Walking under the Ladder," *Esquire* (Feb., 1939): 82.
5. Froh, *Edgar B. Davis and Sequences in Business Capitalism*, p. 9.
6. Ibid., p. 14.
7. Edgar B. Davis, confidential memorandum, 1949, Papers, Genealogical and Historical Society of Caldwell County, Luling, Tex.
8. Riley Froh, "Edgar B. Davis and the United States Rubber Industry with Inclusive Dates," p. 21.
9. E. B. Davis, confidential memorandum, 1949, Papers, Genealogical and Historical Society of Caldwell County.
10. Edgar B. Davis, letter to Robert and Josephine Spurr Weston, Sept. 30, 1932, Papers, Genealogical and Historical Society of Caldwell County.
11. E. B. Davis, confidential memorandum, 1949, Papers, Genealogical and Historical Society of Caldwell County.
12. Ibid.
13. Froh, *Edgar B. Davis and Sequences in Business Capitalism*, pp. 25, 31.
14. Ibid., p. 25.
15. Howard Wolf and Ralph Wolf, *Rubber: A Story of Glory and Greed*, p. 242.
16. E. B. Davis, confidential memorandum, 1949, Papers, Genealogical and Historical Society of Caldwell County.
17. Froh, *Edgar B. Davis*, p. 131.
18. Froh, *Edgar B. Davis and Sequences in Business Capitalism*, pp. 65–66.
19. Froh, *Edgar B. Davis*, p. 133.
20. Froh, *Edgar B. Davis and Sequences in Business Capitalism*, pp. 68–69.
21. Ibid., p. 71.
22. William T. Cameron, *The Cameron Story*, p. 123.
23. E. B. Davis, confidential memorandum, 1949, Papers, Genealogical and Historical Society of Caldwell County.
24. Steve King, "He Gives Away His Millions," *American Magazine* (Aug., 1951): 97.
25. Froh, *Edgar B. Davis and Sequences in Business Capitalism*, p. 72.
26. Davis, *Edgar B. Davis*, pp. 7–8.
27. Froh, *Edgar B. Davis and Sequences in Business Capitalism*, p. 73.
28. Edgar B. Davis, "The Way Out—And On," *North American Review* 234, no. 4 (Oct., 1932): 289.
29. Ibid., p. 290.
30. Eleanor Onderdonk, letter to Edgar B. Davis, May 18, 1946, Papers, Genealogical and Historical Society of Caldwell County.
31. Froh, *Edgar B. Davis*, pp. 89–91.
32. David Figart, personal notes, May 18, 1932, Edgar B. Davis Papers, Genealogical and Historical Society of Caldwell County.
33. Ibid., May 20, 1932.
34. Froh, *Edgar B. Davis*, p. 99.
35. Wolf and Wolf, *Rubber*, p. 245.
36. Froh, *Edgar B. Davis*, p. 10.
37. Ibid., p. 11.
38. Ibid., p. 13.
39. *San Antonio Express-News*, July 2, 1972.
40. Froh, "The Folklore and Facts," pp. 91–92.
41. Froh, *Edgar B. Davis and Sequences in Business Capitalism*, pp. 93, 95.
42. Froh, *Edgar B. Davis*, p. 17.
43. Ibid., p. 22.
44. Ibid., pp. 42–43.
45. Francis W. Wilson, "The Great Picnic," *Plum Creek Almanac* 2, no. 2 (Fall, 1984): 160.
46. Ibid.
47. Froh, *Edgar B. Davis and Sequences in Business Capitalism*, p. 130.
48. *Luling Signal*, Oct. 19, 1951.
49. Frank X. Tolbert, "Wild Flower Wildcatter," *Texas Star* 10 (July 18, 1971): pp. 10–11.
50. Froh, *Edgar B. Davis*, pp. 51–53.
51. Ibid., pp. 55–57.
52. Ibid., p. 62.
53. J. Frank Davis, letter to Edwin C. Hill, May 11, 1934, Papers, Genealogical and Historical Society of Caldwell County.
54. Froh, *Edgar B. Davis*, p. 54.

55. Stanley Walker, "Where Are They Now? Mr. Davis and His Millions," *New Yorker* (Nov. 26, 1949): 40.

56. Ibid.

57. Pemberton, "Walking under the Ladder," p. 83.

58. Walker, "Where Are They Now?," pp. 46–47.

59. Froh, *Edgar B. Davis*, p. 69.

60. King, "He Gives Away His Millions," p. 101.

61. Froh, *Edgar B. Davis and Sequences in Business Capitalism*, p. 151; and "Listing of Performances, 1926–27," Edgar B. Davis Papers, Genealogical and Historical Society of Caldwell County, Luling, Tex.

62. Pemberton, "Walking under the Ladder," p. 155.

63. Grace Davidson, "$10,000 Concert on Every Sunday," Sept., 1929, Edgar B. Davis Papers, Genealogical and Historical Society of Caldwell County.

64. Froh, *Edgar B. Davis*, p. 74.

65. Edgar B. Davis Papers, Genealogical and Historical Society of Caldwell County.

66. Theodore Peterson, *Magazines in the Twentieth Century*, p. 147.

CHAPTER 3.
A CONTEST WORTHY OF FLOWERS

1. Bess Carroll Woolford and Ellen Schulz Quillin, *The Story of the Witte Memorial Museum, 1922–1960*, p. 133.

2. Ibid., p. 147.

3. Steinfeldt, *The Onderdonks*, p. 30.

4. "A Short History of the San Antonio Art League," 1983, San Antonio Art League, San Antonio, Tex., Files, p. 2.

5. Eleanor Onderdonk, "The San Antonio Competitive Exhibitions, 1927–1928–1929," San Antonio Art League Files, p. 1.

6. Helen Raley, "Texas Wild Flower Art Exhibit," *Holland's, The Magazine of the South* 46 (July, 1927): 49.

7. Onderdonk, "The San Antonio Competitive Exhibitions," p. 1.

8. Eleanor Onderdonk, letter to H. Miller Ainsworth, Mar. 30, 1950, Files, Luling Foundation.

9. *San Antonio Express*, Mar. 21, 1926.

10. "The Art League of San Antonio, Texas Offers $6000 in Cash Prizes for Landscapes in Oil Depicting Texas Wildflowers," San Antonio Art League Files, contest rules.

11. San Antonio Art League Files.

12. Ibid.

13. Ibid.

14. *San Antonio Express*, Mar. 21, 1926.

15. *San Antonio Express*, Sept. 19, 1926.

16. Kalil, *The Texas Landscape*, p. 26.

17. *San Antonio Express*, Jan. 27, 1927.

18. "Savants Judge 77 Paintings in Contest," Feb. 18, 1927, San Antonio Art League Files.

19. *Texas Wild Flower Competitive Exhibition*, exhibition catalogue, San Antonio Art League Files.

20. Ibid.

21. Fisk, *A History of Texas Artists and Sculptors*, pp. 177–78.

22. Alexandre Hogue, "That Annual Crop of Texas Wild Flowers," *Southwest Review* XIV, no. 3 (Spring, 1929): 377.

23. *San Antonio Express*, Feb. 10, 1927.

24. *San Antonio Light*, Feb. 2, 1927.

25. "Private Showing of Flower Art," n.d., San Antonio Art League Files.

26. *San Antonio Express*, Feb. 20, 1927.

27. "Dinner for Art Judges," Feb. 19, 1927, San Antonio Art League Files.

28. Fisk, *A History of Texas Artists and Sculptors*, pp. 30–32.

29. Raley, "Texas Wild Flower Art Exhibit," p. 49.

30. Onderdonk, letter to Ainsworth, Mar. 30, 1950, Files, Luling Foundation.

31. Steinfeldt, *Art for History's Sake*, p. 39.

32. D. C. Bradford, letter to Sam Lattimore, Feb. 1, 1978, Papers, Genealogical and Historical Society of Caldwell County.

33. Raley, "Texas Wild Flower Art Exhibit," p. 5.

34. Fisk, *A History of Texas Artists and Sculptors*, p. 29.

35. Raley, "Texas Wild Flower Art Exhibit," p. 5.

36. Artist biography, San Antonio Art League Files.

37. Raley, "Texas Wild Flower Art Exhibit," p. 49.

38. Minutes, San Antonio Art League, Apr. 6, 1927.

39. Raley, "Texas Wild Flower Art Exhibit," p. 5.

40. *San Antonio Light*, Mar. 27, 1927.

41. Minutes, San Antonio Art League, n.d.

42. *San Antonio Light*, Mar. 27, 1927.

43. "World Famous Send Entries into Contest," Feb. 3, 1928, San Antonio Art League Files.

44. Woolford and Quillin, *The Story of the Witte Memorial Museum*, p. 137.

45. "Texas Contest Pictures on Display," Feb. 3, 1928, San Antonio Art League Files.

46. *San Antonio Express*, Feb. 15, 1928.

47. "New Storm Brews in Art Contest Here," Feb. 16, 1928, San Antonio Art League Files.

48. *San Antonio Express*, Feb. 15, 1928.

49. Ibid.

50. Ibid.

51. Ibid.

52. "Cotton to Be Kept in Exhibit," Feb. 16, 1928, San Antonio Art League Files.

53. Press release to *San Antonio Express*, July 1, 1953, San Antonio Art League Files.

54. *San Antonio Express*, Feb. 15, 1928.

55. "Art Turns Spotlight on Us," n.d., San Antonio Art League Files.

56. "Judges Pick Davis Art Winners," Feb. 17, 1928, San Antonio Art League Files.

57. Ibid.

58. Shannon, Dillard Mitchell, *Adrian Brewer: Arkansas Artist*, p. 6.

59. Lilly, "The Texas Wild Flower Painting Competitions," p. 342.

60. Theodore J. Morgan, "In San Antonio's World of Art," n.d., San Antonio Art League Files.

61. Froh, *Edgar B. Davis and Sequences in Business Capitalism*, note 33, pp. 149, 236.

62. "Texas Art," *Time* (Apr. 2, 1928).

63. Clara Caffrey Pancoast, "Riot of Colors Marks Dinner Given by Davis," n.d., San Antonio Art League Files.

64. "$31,500 Prizes Announced by Davis," n.d., San Antonio Art League Files.

65. "Davis Competition Pictures Go East," Mar. 8, 1929, San Antonio Art League files.

66. "Texas Wildflower Paintings to Be Shown in the East," n.d., San Antonio Art League Files.

67. *Abilene Morning News*, Sept. 21, 1928.

68. Lilly, "The Texas Wild Flower Painting Competitions," p. 346.

69. *San Antonio Express*, Feb., 2, 1929.

70. Woolford and Quillin, *The Story of the Witte Memorial Museum*, p. 137.

71. *San Antonio Express*, Feb. 4, 1929.

72. *San Antonio Express*, Feb. 28, 1929.

73. "Art Contest Judges Named," *San Antonio Express*, n.d., San Antonio Art League Files.

74. Lilly, "The Texas Wild Flower Painting Competitions," p. 346.

75. Hogue, "That Annual Crop of Texas Wild Flowers," pp. 377–78.

76. Artist biography, San Antonio Art League Files.

77. *San Antonio Express*, Feb. 1, 1929.

78. Ibid.

79. Kalil, *The Texas Landscape*, p. 26.

80. Lilly, "The Texas Wild Flower Painting Competitions," p. 346.

81. *San Antonio Express*, Feb. 1, 1929.

82. *San Antonio Express*, Feb. 24, 1929.

83. *San Antonio Express*, Mar. 6, 1929.

84. Edgar B. Davis, letter to Eleanor Onderdonk, July 2, 1935, San Antonio Art League Files.

CHAPTER 4.
POSTSCRIPTS AND REFLECTIONS

1. Walker, "Where Are They Now?," p. 36.

2. Froh, *Edgar B. Davis*, pp. 96–102.

3. Ibid., p. 99.

4. Ibid., p. 103.

5. Walker, "Where Are They Now?," p. 35.

6. Froh, *Edgar B. Davis and Sequences in Business Capitalism*, pp. 179–85.

7. Ibid., pp. 187–98.

8. Woolford and Quillin, *The Story of the Witte Memorial Museum*, p. 128.

9. Davis to Onderdonk, July 2, 1935, San Antonio Art League Files.

10. Steinfeldt, *The Onderdonks*, p. 190.

11. *San Antonio Express*, Feb. 2, 1944.

12. "Thistle Blossoms," E. Martin Hennings, Taos, San Antonio Art League Files, p. 2.

13. "A Short History of the San Antonio Art League," 1983, San Antonio Art League Files, p. 2.

14. Walker, "Where Are They Now?," p. 44.

15. King, "He Gives Away His Millions," p. 101.

16. Walker, "Where Are They Now?," p. 37.

17.   Froh, *Edgar B. Davis,* pp. 136–37.

18.   Ibid., pp. 129–36.

19.   Ibid., p. 136.

20.   *Dallas Morning News,* June 24, 1950.

21.   Froh, *Edgar B. Davis,* p. 143.

22.   "Death Comes to Edgar B. Davis," *Magnolia News* (Dec., 1951).

23.   Matthews, *San Antonio Lawyer,* p. 115.

24.   King, "He Gives Away His Millions," p. 24.

25.   Fisk, *A History of Texas Artists and Sculptors,* p. 5.

26.   O'Brien, *Art and Artists of Texas,* p. 12.

27.   Carraro, *Jerry Bywaters,* p. 12.

28.   Edgar B. Davis, "Art and Music," public address, Nov. 7, 1931, San Antonio Art League Files.

29.   Ibid.

30.   Ibid.

31.   Ibid.

Bibliography

Abilene Morning News, September 21, 1928.

Anthony, Marie. "The Davis Art Competition." *Bunker Monthly* 2, no. 1 (July, 1928).

"Art of Texas Presents Epitome of Aesthetics of Modern Age." *Art Digest* (June 1, 1936): 14–15, 20.

Battle, William J. "Art in Texas: An Outline." *Southwest Review* XIV, no. 1 (Autumn, 1928): 51–59.

Bradford, D. C. Papers. Genealogical and Historical Society of Caldwell County, Luling, Texas.

Bywaters, Jerry. *Seventy-Five Years of Art in Dallas.* Dallas: Dallas Museum of Fine Art, 1978.

Cameron, William T. *The Cameron Story.* Tucson: International Society for Vehicle Preservation, 1990.

Carraro, Francine. *Jerry Bywaters: A Life in Art.* Austin: University of Texas Press, 1994.

Chambers, Bruce W. *Art and Artists of the South.* Columbia: University of South Carolina Press, 1984.

Dallas Morning News, June 24, 1950.

Davis, Edgar B. Files. San Antonio Art League, San Antonio, Texas.

———. Papers. Genealogical and Historical Society of Caldwell County, Luling, Texas. This collection includes documents and photographs pertaining to Edgar Davis's work and life in Luling.

———. "The Way Out—And On." *North American Review* 234, no. 4 (October, 1932): 289–91.

Davis, J. Frank. Papers. Genealogical and Historical Society of Caldwell County, Luling, Texas.

Davis, Lincoln K. *Edgar B. Davis: A Native Son Who Never Forgot His Home Town.* Brockton, Mass.: Pilgrim Foundation, 1983.

"Death Comes to Edgar B. Davis." *Magnolia News* (December, 1951).

Figart, David. Personal notes regarding Edgar Davis. June 30, 1931–March 3, 1933. Edgar B. Davis Papers. Genealogical and Historical Society of Caldwell County

Fisk, Frances Battaile. *A History of Texas Artists and Sculptors.* Abilene, Tex.: Fisk Publishing, 1928.

Foree, Kenneth. *Citizen of Luling.* Luling, Tex.: Magnolia Petroleum Company, 1947.

Froh, Riley. *Edgar B. Davis: Wildcatter Extraordinary.* Luling, Tex.: Luling Foundation, 1984.

———. *Edgar B. Davis and Sequences in Business Capitalism: From Shoes to Rubber to Oil.* New York and London: Garland Publishing, 1993.

———. "Edgar B. Davis and the United States Rubber Industry with Inclusive Dates. Master's thesis, Southwest Texas State College, 1968.

———. "The Folklore and Facts behind the Luling Discovery Well." *Plum Creek Almanac* 2, no. 2 (Fall, 1984): 89–98.

"Glory of the Morning." *Pioneer Magazine* 7 (April, 1927): 5, 12.

Goetzmann, William H., and Becky Duval Reese. *Texas Images and Visions.* Austin: University of Texas Press, 1983.

Goetzmann, William H., and William N. Goetzmann. *The West of the*

Imagination. New York and London: W. W. Norton and Company, 1986.

Goodrich, Lloyd, and John I. H. Baur. *American Art of Our Century.* New York: Praeger, 1961.

Hogue, Alexandre. "That Annual Crop of Texas Wild Flowers." *Southwest Review* XIV, no. 3 (Spring, 1929): 377–78.

Hoskinson, Jo, and Vera Holding. "The Unforgettable Edgar B. Davis." *Drilling* (February, 1976): 22–29.

Kalil, Susie. *The Texas Landscape, 1900–1986.* Houston: Museum of Fine Arts, 1986.

King, Steve. "He Gives Away His Millions." *American Magazine* (August, 1951): 24–25, 96–101.

Lilly, Marie Seacord. "The Texas Wild Flower Painting Competitions." *American Magazine of Art* XX (June, 1929): 342–47.

Luling Signal, November 10, 1950.

———, October 19, 1951.

Matthews, Wilbur L. *San Antonio Lawyer: Memoranda of Cases and Clients.* San Antonio: Corona Publishing, 1983.

Mitchell, Shannon Dillard. *Adrian Brewer: Arkansas Artist.* Little Rock: University of Arkansas at Little Rock, Department of Art, 1996.

Moore, Sylvia. *No Bluebonnets, No Yellow Roses: Essays on Texas Women in the Arts.* New York: Midmarch Arts Press, 1988.

Murray, Marion. "Art in the Southwest." *Southwest Review* 12, no. 4 (July, 1926): 281–93.

O'Brien, Esse Forrester. *Art and Artists of Texas.* Dallas: Tardy Publishing Company, 1935.

Onderdonk, Eleanor. Files. Luling Foundation, Luling, Texas.

———. Papers. Genealogical and Historical Society of Caldwell County, Luling, Texas.

Palmer, Carlton. Files. Luling Foundation, Luling, Texas.

Pemberton, Murdock. "Walking under the Ladder." *Esquire* (February, 1939): 82–83, 155–57.

Peterson, Theodore. *Magazines in the Twentieth Century.* Urbana: University of Illinois Press, 1964.

Pinckney, Pauline A. *Painting in Texas: The Nineteenth Century.* Austin: University of Texas Press, 1967.

Raley, Helen. "Texas Wild Flower Art Exhibit." *Holland's, The Magazine of the South* 46 (July, 1927): 5, 49.

Ratcliffe, Sam Deshong. *Painting Texas History to 1900.* Austin: University of Texas Press, 1992.

Samuels, Harold, and Peggy Samuels. *The Illustrated Biographical Encyclopedia of Artists of the American West.* New York: Doubleday and Company, 1976.

San Antonio Art League, San Antonio, Texas. Files. Texas Wildflower Competitive Exhibitions, 1927–1929. This collection contains news accounts, correspondence, and other documents related to the Texas Wildflower Competitive Exhibitions. The collection contains files on the paintings of the Davis Collection and notes on the artists.

———. Minutes.

San Antonio Express, March 21–September 19, 1926.

———, January 27–February 20, 1927.

———, February 15, 1928.

———, February 1–March 6, 1929.

———, February 2, 1944.

San Antonio Express-News, July 2, 1972.

San Antonio Light, February 2–March 27, 1927.

Smith, Goldie Capers. *The Creative Arts in Texas: A Handbook of Biography.* Nashville/Dallas: Cokesbury Press, 1926.

Steinfeldt, Cecilia. *Art for History's Sake: The Texas Collection of the Witte Museum.* San Antonio: Texas State Historical Association, 1993.

———. "Blooming Bluebonnets: A Texas Tradition." *Southwest Art* 14 (April, 1985): 62–69.

———. *The Onderdonks: A Family of Texas Painters.* San Antonio: Trinity University Press, 1976.

Stern, Jean, and Janet Dominik. *Masterworks of California Impressionism.* Phoenix: FFCA Publishing Company, 1986.

"Texas Art," *Time* (April 2, 1928).

Tolbert, Frank X. "Wild Flower Wildcatter." *Texas Star* 10 (July 18, 1971): 10–11.

Trenton, Patricia, ed. *Independent Spirits: Women Painters of the American West, 1890–1945.* Los Angeles: University of California Press, 1995.

Walker, Stanley. "Where Are They Now? Mr. Davis and His Millions." *New Yorker* (November 26, 1949): 35–49.

Wilbanks, Elsie Montgomery. *Art on the Texas Plains.* Lubbock: South Plains Art Guild, 1959.

Wilson, Francis W. "The Great Picnic." *Plum Creek Almanac* 2, no. 2 (Fall, 1984): 160–61.

Wolf, Howard, and Ralph Wolf. *Rubber: A Story of Glory and Greed.* New York: Covici-Friede Publishers, 1936.

Woolford, Bess Carroll, and Ellen Schulz Quillin. *The Story of the Witte Memorial Museum, 1922–1960.* San Antonio: San Antonio Museum Association, 1966.

Index

Note: Pages with illustrations are indicated in **boldface** type. Color plates are not indexed, but are listed in the frontmatter.